Home Cooking IN A HURRY
Sarah Howell

BROADMAN PRESS
Nashville, Tennessee

© Copyright 1985 • Broadman Press
All rights reserved
4270-02
ISBN: 0-8054-7002-6

Dewey Decimal Classification: 641.5
Subject Heading: COOKERY
Library of Congress Catalog Card Number: 84-24246
Printed in the United States of America

Unless otherwise noted, all Scripture quotations are taken from the *Good News Bible*, the Bible in Today's English Version. Old Testament: Copyright © American Bible Society 1976; New Testament: Copyright © American Bible Society 1966, 1971, 1976. Used by permission.

Library of Congress Cataloging in Publication Data

Howell, Sarah, 1929-
  Home cooking in a hurry.

  Includes index.
  1. Cookery. I. Title.
TX715.H8618   1985   641.5′55   84-24246
ISBN 0-8054-7002-6

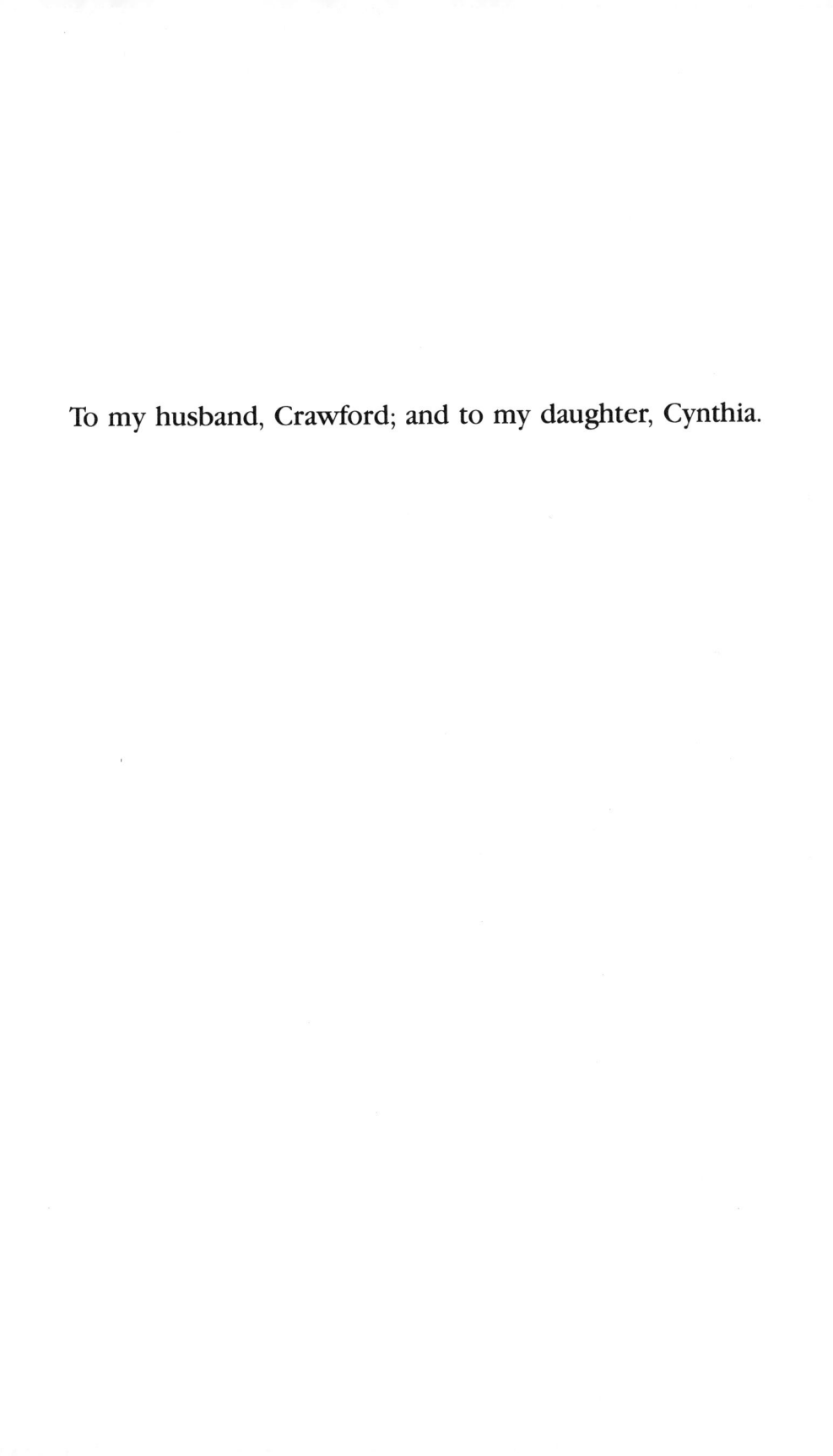

To my husband, Crawford; and to my daughter, Cynthia.

Introduction

"Ordinary people think merely how they will spend their time; a man of intellect tries to use it."—*Wisdom of Life,* 1845.

This book came about from need and practical experience. As a busy wife and mother with professional interests, I have had limited time to spend in the kitchen. Yet I enjoy cooking and entertaining and want my home to be a warm and loving place. The answer has been to develop menus and recipes that are good—and good for you—which can be prepared in a hurry.

Each of us receives a precious gift every day—twenty-four hours. Have you ever thought that all human beings receive the same amount of time? But my, how differently they use it! Some people invest time in ways that they accomplish much for themselves and others, while others waste so much time that little or nothing is produced.

People who live in a home create the atmosphere. Today, as always, people cherish family and friends and wish they had more time to spend sharing a well-cooked meal with them. The dining table can be an oasis, a meeting place for the family—a place that nourishes physically and emotionally. Eating with loved ones offers opportunity for communion.

"They eat, they drink, and in communion sweet quaff immortality and joy" (Milton, *Paradise Lost,* 1674).

This book is for those busy people who want to make use of time spent in the kitchen, so they and their families will not miss the joys of home cooking and warm hospitality; people who want good, delicious food on the table with the least amount of time and effort; people who want to manage time instead of time and events managing them.

Contents

1. **How to Use This Book**	11
2. **Meals in Minutes—Menus and Recipes**	15
3. **Essence of Herbs and Spices**	103
Sensible Seasoning	104
Herb and Seasoning Chart	107
Suggested Herbs and Spices to Keep on Hand	113
4. **A Balanced Diet—A Balanced Life**	114
The Balanced Diet	114
Food Guide for Balanced Diet	115
Weight Control and Exercise	116
The Balanced Life	116
5. **Company Coming**	117
Planning for Company	118
Company Cooking	118
Menus and Recipes	122
Seated Dinners	122
Buffet Service	129
Luncheons	136
Outdoor Entertaining	142
6. **Definitions of Cooking Terms**	147
7. **Weights and Measures**	153

8. **Food Equivalents** 154

9. **Make Do** 156

   Index 158

1
How to Use This Book

Meals in Minutes—Menus

No more "What shall we eat tonight?" Good meals don't just happen. Meals must be planned even with "quick to prepare" foods. These menus are designed to save the reader time with meal planning. The foods listed in each menu go well together. The tastes, textures, and colors of these foods harmonize to produce nutritious, delicious meals in minutes.

There are menus for various types of meals—from "super speedy" to dinners for company. Most of the meals can be prepared in less than forty-five minutes. Many can be prepared in fifteen or twenty minutes. I am not giving exact cooking times, though, because an experienced cook can prepare a meal faster than a novice. Also, anyone preparing a meal the second time should prepare it in less time than the first.

With limited time, and no outside help, home-cooked meals can become adequate, but dull. Not these meals! Eat with pleasure—in minutes.

If you have a food (perhaps a jar of dried beef or some leftover ham), and want a planned menu for its use, look in the Index under the name of that food.

You will find that some menus offer a choice of desserts. One can be prepared in a short time, and another is "super speedy." When time is really limited, use the second choice. If watching calories, you might want to eliminate dessert altogether. I do hope you will try some of these goodies, though.

The menus do not list beverages since there would be too much repetition with suggestions. Choices are left to the reader.

Few bread recipes are included since there are many delicious ones on the market. A person with little time would do well to check bakery breads, as well as refrigerated, frozen, and prepared mixes at the grocery. Several bread recipes which have been included use purchased bread in a novel way—changing taste for the better.

Meals in Minutes—Recipes

Mouth-watering recipes that taste good, look good, and are good for you are listed. If you delight in good home-cooked food, you will love these quick-to-prepare foods.

To save time, recipes are listed with menus—no searching through files for meat, vegetables, desserts, etc. If you want a recipe for a certain food, chicken for instance, look in the Index under chicken. There will be numerous recipes using chicken.

Index

Foods are listed in alphabetical order in the Index (angel cake, appetizers, apples, applesauce, etc.). Also, foods are listed by categories (cakes, meats, pies, salads, etc.).

A wide variety of subjects are also listed by name and categories (dinners, entertaining, herbs, ingredient substitutions, luncheons, nutrition, seasonings, weights and measures, etc.).

Essence of Herbs and Spices

Cooking with herbs and spices is not complicated or time consuming. Their use makes food tastier and more appealing to the eye and appetite. This chapter presents information about how to give simple food a gourmet touch with seasoning.

The reader will find an Herb and Seasoning Chart. The chart is different from most since it first lists foods which you might be cooking, not herbs and spices. All a cook has to do is locate a food on the chart, then see what seasonings go well with it. This saves an enormous amount of time.

A Balanced Diet—A Balanced Life
A discussion on basic nutrition and what foods need to be eaten daily for good health.

Company Coming
Hosts will find information at their fingertips about planning meals for guests. Numerous menus and recipes for company dinners and luncheons are given as well as suggestions for their service.

There is a list of foods and amounts you will need in order to serve twelve or twenty-five people.

Charts
Several informative, time-saving charts are given:
1. Definitions of Cooking Terms
2. Weights and Measures
3. Food Equivalents
    Utilize this list (regardless how many people will be served) for fast location of amounts of food needed for a meal.
4. Make-Do
    If you run out of a food item and need it in a hurry, look at this list and find a substitute.

2
Meals in Minutes
Menus and Recipes

Broiled Ham Slice
Broiler Asparagus   Broiled Pineapple
Strawberry Doughnut

An elegance with ease meal. Cooking time for this broiler meal is 16 minutes, and there is only one pan to wash.

Broiler Asparagus

Open one can (desired size) asparagus. Place vegetable and liquid in bottom of broiler pan; salt lightly. Place broiler rack over asparagus. Follow directions below to cook ham.

Broiled Ham Slice

1 center cut slice, tendered, ham

Cut fat around edge in several places to prevent curling (leave fat on). Place on broiler rack. Broil 7-8 minutes 3 inches from heat. Turn meat; add sliced pineapple (see directions that follow); broil 7-8 minutes.

Broiled Pineapple

1 slice pineapple per serving
1 tablespoon butter, melted

Brown sugar to sprinkle

Drain pineapple; place on broiler rack. Brush with butter; sprinkle brown sugar on top. Broil until lightly brown on top.

Strawberry Doughnuts

1 doughnut per serving

2-3 teaspoons strawberry jam per serving

Split doughnuts in half horizontally. Spread jam on cut sides. Broil one minute. Sprinkle with confectioners sugar before serving, if desired.

It is better to dwell in the wilderness, than with a contentious and an angry woman.

Proverbs 21:19

Turkey Breast Steaks I
Steamed Green Peas
Mandarin Orange-Carrot Salad
Cranberry Spice Cake
(or purchase cake)

A mouth watering, nutritious meal with preparation time (excluding dessert) of thirty minutes or less.

When starting the main part of the meal, prepare the salad first. Set it in the refrigerator until time to serve. Next put the peas on to steam; then cook the meat.

It would be a good idea to set the table first since the food is cooked before you know it.

Turkey Breast Steaks I

Look in the poultry section of your grocery for sliced turkey breast. Sometimes it is called turkey steaks, other times turkey tenderloin.

6-8 turkey steak slices
3 tablespoons cooking oil
2 tablespoons butter or margarine
Salt and pepper to taste

¾ teaspoon celery seed
3 tablespoons lemon juice
½ teaspoon sage
2 tablespoons parsley, chopped

Rinse turkey in cold water. Drain; pat dry with paper towel. Sprinkle salt, pepper, and celery seed on meat.

Heat oil and butter in frying pan. Add turkey steaks. Cook steaks 2-3 minutes on each side (meat turns white). Remove to platter. To the drippings left in the pan add lemon juice, sage, and parsley. Scrape drippings from pan and stir; pour over meat. Serves 4.

Steamed Green Peas

1 package (10 oz.) frozen green peas
⅛ teaspoon celery seed
½ teaspoon salt
Dash of pepper

4 or 5 leaves of lettuce
1 teaspoon sugar
2 tablespoons butter
1 tablespoon parsley, chopped
1 tablespoon chives, chopped

Cover bottom of pan with lettuce leaves. Break frozen peas apart; place on top of lettuce. Sprinkle other ingredients on top of peas. Cover tightly; cook on low heat approximately 15 minutes. Serves 4. These peas are beautifully green and delicious.

Mandarin Orange-Carrot Salad

1 can (11 oz.) Mandarin orange segments
3 or 4 carrots, shredded
¼ cup raisins

1 teaspoon lemon juice
3 or 4 tablespoons mayonnaise
Lettuce leaves

Combine all ingredients except lettuce; chill. Serve on lettuce leaves.

Cranberry Spice Cake

1 box spice cake mix
1 can (16 oz.) whole berry cranberry sauce

¼ cup lemon juice
1 tablespoon honey
Whipped topping

Combine cranberry sauce, lemon juice, and honey. Grease bottom and sides of a 10½ x 14 inch pan. Spread cranberry sauce mixture on bottom of pan. Following package directions, prepare cake for baking. Pour over cranberry mixture in pan. Bake until it springs back when touched—approximately 45 minutes. Remove from oven. Serve as upside down cake. Add a dollop of whipped topping to each serving.

Help us so that we may give
Beauty to the lives we live.
Let Thy love and let Thy grace
Shine upon our dwelling place.

    Edgar A. Guest

Turkey Breast Steaks II
Pan Broiled Mushrooms
Julienne Carrots
Kiwi-Grapefruit-Apple Wedge Salad

This gourmet meal can be prepared and on the table in thirty minutes.

Turkey Breast Steaks II

Buy (fresh or frozen) sliced turkey breast or tenderloin. It is ready to cook—quickly.

4 slices turkey breast	1 teaspoon celery seeds
1 tablespoon butter	½ teaspoon salt
1 tablespoon cooking oil	Dash of pepper

Shake seasonings on turkey. Melt fat in skillet. Sauté first side 3 minutes; turn; fry 2 minutes on other side. Serves 4.

Pan Broiled Mushrooms

Use the same skillet used for the turkey steaks. No need to wash it; turkey and mushroom flavors blend beautifully.

1 (4½ oz.) jar mushrooms
2 tablespoons butter
Dash seasoned salt
Dash pepper

Melt butter over medium heat. Drain liquid from mushrooms. Sauté mushrooms in butter (about 4 minutes). Add seasoned salt and pepper. Serve over turkey breast. (Pan broiled mushrooms are also delicious over beef, veal, and pork.)

Julienne Carrots

4 or 5 carrots
2 tablespoons butter
½ teaspoon salt
1 tablespoon water
Dash of ginger or mace
1 teaspoon sugar, brown or white

Wash and scrape carrots. Grate or very thinly slice. Melt butter; add other ingredients; stir. Cover tightly; simmer 5-8 minutes. Serves 4.

Kiwi-Grapefruit-Apple Wedge Salad

1 grapefruit, sectioned, or use canned sections
1 large red delicious apple
1 kiwi

Peel kiwi; slice into round slices. Core and section apple; leave peel on. Arrange fruits on lettuce. Alternate the green kiwi, red apple, and grapefruit for eye appeal.

Seafood Tomatoes
Cheese Biscuits
Sherbet

A simple salad meal, ideal for summer. The seafood mixture can be prepared ahead of time if you wish. Stuff the tomatoes at the last minute.

Seafood Tomatoes

4 medium-sized tomatoes
1½ cups cooked seafood (lobster, shrimp, crab, or a mixture of all three)
⅓ cup mayonnaise
1 tablespoon lemon juice
¼ teaspoon celery seed
½ teaspoon dill weed
½ teaspoon salt

Mix all ingredients except tomatoes; set aside. Peel tomatoes; cut off ¼ inch from the stem end. Slice tomatoes into vertical slices (top to bottom), not quite through, forming a flower shape. Place tomatoes on salad greens. Fill with seafood mixture. Sprinkle paprika on top. Serves 4.

Cheese Biscuits

1 can refrigerated biscuits   Cheddar cheese

Cut Cheddar cheese into 1-inch cubes. Open refrigerated biscuits. With hands press out each biscuit to 1/8 inch thick. Place one cheese square on each flattened biscuit. Wrap biscuit dough around each cheese square and press down with fingers to seal in cheese. Bake in 475° oven until nicely browned. Serve hot.

A house is built of logs and stone,
   Of tiles and posts and piers;
A home is built of loving deeds
   That stand a thousand years.

                              Victor Hugo, 1802-1885

Broiled Steak
Broiled Tomatoes   **Broiler Green Beans**
Tossed Green Salad
Apricot Whip
(or purchase dessert)

A sizzling steak dinner takes 20 minutes cooking time and leaves one pan to wash—if you purchase dessert.

Broiler Green Beans

These canned beans pick up the good flavor from meat drippings and tomatoes.

1 can green beans (any desired size)

Place beans and liquid in bottom of broiler pan; salt lightly. Place broiler rack over beans. Follow directions below to cook steak and tomatoes.

Broiled Steak

If you like rare meat and have a thin cut, broil close to heat. Thicker cuts are cooked farther from heat. Meat which is 1 to 1½ inches thick is usually more juicy than thin steak. One large steak might be better for 2-4 people than small individual ones.

Steaks 1 to 1½ inch thick, sirloin, T-bone, tenderloin, club, or Porterhouse
1-2 tablespoons margarine per steak
Seasoned salt

Place steak on broiler rack; dot with margarine. Broil 4-5 minutes; salt; turn. Dot that side with margarine; salt lightly; broil until sufficiently cooked.

Broiled Tomatoes

1 small tomato, or ½ large per serving
1-2 tablespoons margarine
1 tablespoon basil, chopped
1-2 tablespoons chives, chopped
1-2 tablespoons parsley, chopped
½ teaspoon salt

Leave skins on tomatoes. Cut large ones in half; broil cut side up. Small ones are cooked whole. Cut blossom end off, and score tops of small tomatoes. Melt margarine; add seasonings to fat. Place tomatoes on broiler rack; pour fat over tops. Broil 5 minutes.

Apricot Whip

This is a delicious, nutritious dessert—worth the few extra minutes it takes to prepare it.

1 jar (7¾ oz.) junior food, apricots with tapioca
1 cup whipping cream
1-2 tablespoons sugar

Whip cream; fold in apricots and sugar. Turn into sherbet glasses. Keep refrigerated until serving time.

Tomato Rose Salad
Carrot Strips
Hot Buttered Pumpernickel Slices
Peanut Brittle Ice Cream

A great meal in minutes for a hot summer day. Add canned potato sticks to menu if you like.

Tomato Rose Salad

4 medium tomatoes	1 avocado
1⅓ cup cottage cheese	1 tablespoon lemon juice
Salt	Paprika

Slice stem end from tomatoes. Cut each tomato into wedges, forming a star shape—do not cut all the way through the base. Sprinkle with salt; drain upside down. Peel avocado; cut into bite-size pieces; toss in lemon juice (this prevents the avocado from turning dark). Drain avocado; toss with cottage cheese. Place each tomato on lettuce leaf on serving plate. Fill with avocado and cheese mixture. Sprinkle paprika on top. Serves 4. Suggestion: Place tomato rose, carrot strips, and potato sticks on luncheon plates. Pass hot bread—no serving dishes to wash.

Carrot Strips

2 carrots

Wash carrots; scrape. Slice into julienne strips 2-3 inches long. Keep in ice water until time to serve. Drain and serve.

Hot Buttered Pumpernickel Slices

Lightly butter bread slices. Wrap with aluminum foil. Heat in 350° oven until just warm.

Peanut Brittle Ice Cream

| ½ cup peanut brittle, finely crushed | 1 quart vanilla ice cream |

Combine crushed peanut brittle with slightly softened ice cream. Keep in freezer until time to serve.

Vanilla Sugar
Vanilla sugar gives a gourmet touch to hot tea and all kinds of fruits—fresh peaches, strawberries, pears, raspberries, applesauce.

To make vanilla sugar split one vanilla bean; place with sugar in covered sugar bowl or small canister for two weeks—to age. It is also delicious in whipped cream and puddings.

Fried Country Ham
Red-Eye Gravy
Grits   Vegetable Tray
(see Index)
Biscuits   Butter
Jelly, Jam, or Sorghum Syrup

A real "down home" country dinner in minutes. It makes my mouth water to think about it.

You can make biscuits if you have time, but there are a lot of good ones on the market to purchase.

Have you ever had sorghum syrup made on the farm from sorghum cane? My grandfather made it on his farm. There is a limited supply these days, but it is available and is a very nutritious sweet.

Grits

Three-minute grits

Follow directions on package.

Fried Country Ham

Smoked country ham, cut ¼ to ⅜ inch thick

If there is rind on ham slices, remove. *Do not* remove fat. Score fat to prevent curling. Place in frying pan. Cook on moderate heat—not high—on one side until lightly browned; turn; cook on other side. *Do not overcook.* Ham requires very short cooking time since it has been smoked 9-12 months.

Red-Eye Gravy

After ham has cooked in frying pan and been removed to platter, add 2-3 tablespoons water to pan drippings. Bring to boil, scraping pan while stirring continuously. Pour over ham, or serve in gravy boat.

Better is a dinner of herbs where love is, than a stalled ox and hatred therewith.

Proverbs 15:17

Vegetable Juice Cocktail
Baked Chicken Salad
Honeydew Melon

A super speedy meal—requires 12-15 minutes cooking time. It is also a great "planned-over meal" using leftover chicken or turkey.

Vegetable Juice Cocktail

2 cups tomato or vegetable juice
1 teaspoon celery seed or basil
Dash hot pepper sauce
1 teaspoon Worcestershire sauce

Combine ingredients. Serve cold. Serves 4.

Baked Chicken Salad
(may be prepared ahead of time)

1½ to 2 cups cooked chicken or turkey
1½ cups diced celery
2 tablespoons lemon juice
⅓ cup salted peanuts
1 teaspoon onion flakes
¼ teaspoon salt
¾ cup mayonnaise
½ cup cheddar cheese, grated

Cut chicken into 1-inch pieces. Combine all ingredients except cheese. Put into buttered casserole dish. Sprinkle cheese on top. Bake 12-15 minutes in 450° oven. Serves 3-4.

Honeydew Melon

Slice melon into wedges. Serve plain or topped with other fruit—fresh cherries, strawberries.

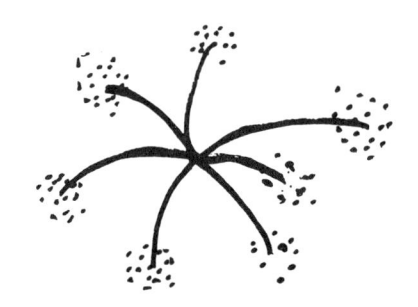

Time-Saving Work Habits

1. Keep work space clear—put things away as soon as you're finished with them.
2. If pans have food stuck to them, soak in soapy water soon as emptied.
3. The assembly-line method speeds food preparation. Place all ingredients to be used out on a counter before starting to cook. Preparation of food should be one continuous operation—no stopping to hunt for an ingredient.

Save steps when setting the table. Carry food and dishes on a tray or tea cart.

When peeling vegetables and fruits, work over paper. To clean up, toss peels and paper in garbage.

Scrumptious Catfish
Corn-filled Tomatoes
Spinach Salad
Peach Puff

Heat oven to 350°. Prepare cake first. Get it into oven while you prepare the other food.

Scrumptious Catfish

If you think catfish is a lowly fish, just try this!

4 skinned, pan-dressed catfish	½ teaspoon dill, chopped
⅓ cup margarine, melted	½ teaspoon basil, chopped
1 cup bread crumbs	2 tablespoons parsley, chopped
⅔ cup Parmesan cheese, grated	1½ teaspoons salt
1 teaspoon paprika	

Mix all ingredients except fish and margarine in a bag. Dip fish into melted margarine; then shake (gently) in bag to coat with crumb mixture. Bake in buttered, shallow casserole until juicy tender—30-40 minutes; in 350° oven. Serves 4. Hint: Fish may be prepared ahead of time and kept refrigerated until time to cook.

Corn-filled Tomatoes

4 medium tomatoes
1 (16 oz.) can cream-style corn
1 clove garlic (mashed)
1½ tablespoons butter

½ teaspoon salt
¼ teaspoon pepper
1 teaspoon basil

Remove top, and scoop out center of each tomato. Heat other ingredients 1-2 minutes. Fill center of tomatoes with corn mixture. Bake at 350° until tomatoes are tender but firm—about 15-20 minutes. Serves 4.

Spinach Salad

Fresh spinach, washed, drained, chilled
1 can French fried onions

¼ cup Italian dressing
Salt and pepper to taste

Heat onions in oven to warm. Break spinach into bite-sized pieces, removing stems. Toss all ingredients; serve cold.

Peach Puff

A super simple cake which requires no mixing.

1 (18½ oz.) box yellow cake mix
1 (29 oz.) can sliced peaches with juice

¼ cup water
5 tablespoons butter or margarine, melted

Butter 9 x 13 inch pan. Sprinkle dry cake mix on bottom of pan; spread out. Pour sliced peaches and liquid over dry cake mix (no need to mix). Drizzle melted fat over top. Bake approximately 45 minutes in a 350° oven. A soft lightly brown cake puff forms on top of the peaches.

Sukiyaki
Rice
Purchased Almond Cookies
Green Tea

A Sukiyaki (soo-kee-yah-kee) party is an easy, informal way to entertain. Traditionally, Sukiyaki is cooked at the table in an hibachi. An electric skillet, wok, or regular frying pan will do just as well. The cooking is fast and short, so foods stay crisp and crunchy. It is best to cook the Sukiyaki in two batches, half the ingredients at a time. If more is needed, keep repeating the process.

A few things need to be remembered: (1) Meat should be cut almost tissue-paper thin against the grain; (2) vegetables should be julienned or sliced thin; (3) prepare all ingredients before starting to cook; (4) arrange on a large platter, keeping each item separate—a beautiful sight on a tray; (5) do not crowd the pan; cook seconds.

Sukiyaki

1 pound sirloin beef, sliced paper thin
2 cups carrots, cut julienned strips 2 inches long

Sauce:
⅓ cup soy sauce
3 tablespoons sugar
2 tablespoons lemon juice

2 cups sliced fresh mushrooms or 10 oz. drained, canned
2 cups celery, sliced or julienned
1 cup sliced green onions leaving 3 inches of their tops on, or 1 cup sliced
½ cup green pepper, cut into ½ inch cubes
1 cup bean sprouts (mung)
¼ cup cooking oil
½ cup beef broth or bouillion
Spinach (approximately 1 handful per serving)

The ingredients can be varied to fit your taste. Other foods good in Sukiyaki are tofu and bamboo shoots.

Mix sauce; set aside. Place pan over medium heat; add oil. Add sliced onion; allow to soften; add beef in a single layer and cook until it just loses pinkness; push to side of pan. Add all other ingredients except spinach; stir; cover. Cook 6-8 minutes. Put spinach on top; cook until wilted but still bright green. Serve from cooking pan with rice. Serves 6.

Be not forgetful to entertain strangers: for thereby some have entertained angels unawares.

Hebrews 13:2

Cream will whip faster if bowl and beater are cold. A small amount of lemon juice also helps.

Veal Scallopini
Italian Green Beans
Pink Pear Salad
Coffee Mousse

An Italian or French bread of your choice would be good.

Veal Scallopini

1¼ pounds veal cutlet
2 tablespoons butter
2 tablespoons cooking oil
⅓ cup flour
½ teaspoon salt

1 tablespoon parsley, chopped
3 tablespoons lemon juice
2 tablespoons Parmesan cheese

Have butcher slice cutlets as thinly as possible. Pound very thin with meat cleaver or edge of saucer. Mix flour, salt, parsley. Toss veal in seasoned flour. Warm fat in frying pan over medium heat. Sauté meat until just brown (about 2 minutes) on one side; then brown on other side. Remove to a heatproof platter; add juice to pan drippings. Scrape and stir juice in the pan. Pour over meat. Sprinkle with Parmesan cheese. Run under broiler just to heat. Serves 4.

Italian Green Beans

1 (1 lb.) can Italian green beans
1 tablespoon butter
3 tablespoons Parmesan
   cheese, grated

¼ teaspoon garlic salt
¼ teaspoon paprika

   Heat green beans in liquid to boil. Drain off liquid; add seasonings. Toss lightly. Serves 4.

Pink Pear Salad
(may be prepared ahead of time)

4 large pear halves
Red or green food coloring

4 tablespoons cream or cottage
   cheese
Dash of ginger

   Drain pears. Brush with food coloring. Mix cheese with ginger. Place pear half on lettuce leaf, cut side up on salad plate. Fill center with cheese mixture.

Coffee Mousse
(may be prepared ahead of time)

1 cup hot coffee
24 marshmallows

1 cup chocolate ice cream
1 cup cream, whipped or
   whipped topping

   Melt marshmallows (faster if cut into small pieces) in hot coffee. Let cool. Fold marshmallow mixture into whipped cream and slightly softened ice cream. Pour into compotes. Top with nuts or grated chocolate bar if desired. Keep in freezer until serving time.

Baked Ham Slices
Tomato-Cottage Cheese Salad
Crackers   Potato Chips
Purchased Cake

A meal in minutes. Buy thin sliced ham; serve it with salad, potato chips, and crackers on dinner plates—no serving plates to wash.

Tomato-Cottage Cheese Salad

2 tomatoes (medium size)
½ cup cottage cheese
2 tablespoons sour cream
¼ teaspoon salt
1 tablespoon chives, chopped
2 tablespoons cucumber, peeled and chopped
Paprika

Scoop out center of each tomato. Drain tomatoes upside down. Combine other ingredients except paprika. Stuff tomatoes with cheese mixture. Sprinkle paprika on top. Serves 2.

Curried Chicken
Ramen Noodles
Waldorf Salad
Strawberry Cream

This meal could be prepared in thirty minutes.
Ramen (rah-men) noodles are instant Oriental noodles. Look for them on the grocery shelf with Oriental foods.

Curried Chicken

1 cup diced cooked chicken
1 can (11 oz.) condensed mushroom soup
½ cup milk
¼ to ½ teaspoon curry powder (amount depends on your taste)
2 tablespoons pimientos, chopped

Heat all ingredients except meat to boiling point; simmer 2-3 minutes. Add diced chicken. Serve over noodles. Serves 2. This chicken is also good over toast points.

Ramen Noodles

3-ounce package ramen noodles
1¼ cups water

Remove seasoning mix from package. Boil water; add noodles. Simmer 3 minutes. Use fork to separate noodles and stir. Add seasoning mix. Pour onto a platter, forming a well in the center. Fill center with curried chicken. Serves 2.

Waldorf Salad

1 unpeeled red apple, seeds removed and diced
2 tablespoons celery, diced

2 tablespoons raisins
2 tablespoons mayonnaise
Dash salt

Toss ingredients. Serves 2.

Strawberry Cream

½ cup strawberries, fresh or frozen
2 tablespoons sugar if berries are fresh

1 pint vanilla ice cream

Put ingredients in blender; whip. Store in freezer. Serve slightly softened.

Make use of time, let not advantage slip;
Beauty with itself should not be wasted;
Fair flowers that are not gather'd in their prime,
Rot and consume themselves in little time.
Shakespeare, *Venus and Adonis,* 1593

Shrimp Soup
Crackers or Hot Bread
Banana Boat Salad
Cake
(purchased)

A nutritious and delicious 15-minute meal. Ideal for a busy day.

Shrimp Soup

1 can (10¾ oz.) cream of shrimp soup
3 tablespoons lemon juice
1 medium tomato (chopped)
1 tablespoon parsley (chopped)
¼ teaspoon dill weed
1 cup cooked shrimp (frozen, fresh, canned)
Dash salt
Dash pepper

Place all ingredients, except shrimp, in saucepan; simmer 5-6 minutes. Add shrimp; cook on low heat 3 minutes. (Do not overcook shrimp; it can become tough.) Pour into bowls. Serves 2. Hint: When preparing soup, if it seems too thick, add a small amount water.

Banana Boat Salad

1 banana per serving **Fresh or frozen berries**
Lettuce

Peel and slice bananas lengthwise (as for banana split). On each salad plate place lettuce and two banana slices. Fill boat center with berries.

He that eateth well drinketh well, he that drinketh well sleepeth well, he that sleepeth well sinneth not, and he that sinneth not goeth straight . . . to Paradise.

William Lithgow, 1609

Minute Steak—Creole Style
Banana-Peanut Butter Salad
Pound Cake with Ice Cream

Minute Steak—Creole Style

4 minute steaks
2 tablespoons fat
1 cup uncooked rice
2 cups tomato juice or soup
1 teaspoon basil

1 teaspoon salt
½ teaspoon pepper
1 medium bell pepper, sliced
1 medium onion, sliced

Brown steaks in fat; drain fat from pan. Combine tomato juice, rice, salt, basil, and pepper; pour over steaks. Place onion and pepper rings on top. Cover pan; turn heat to high until steam escapes from lid; turn to simmer. Cook 40-45 minutes. Serves 4.

Banana-Peanut Butter Salad

2-3 bananas, cut in circles
Lettuce

3 tablespoons peanut butter

Arrange lettuce on salad plates. Form a ring with banana circles; fill ring with dollop of peanut butter. Serves 4.

Pound Cake with Ice Cream

Purchase pound cake; top with ice cream of your choice.

Heavenly Father, bless us,
And keep us all alive,
There's ten of us to dinner
And not enough for five.

                                      Unknown, Hodges Grace

Fettucini Sausage Sweet-Sour Red Cabbage
Melon Circles with Lime Sherbet

This meal could be prepared in 30 minutes. Italian bread would be good.

Sausage

Pan fry slowly 15-20 minutes. Drain on paper towel.

Fettucini

Fettucini (Fet′-tu-ci′-ni) is a narrow strip pasta. Small spaghetti can be substituted in recipe.

7 oz. fettucini

Sauce:
¼ cup butter, melted
⅓ cup Parmesan cheese
2 tablespoons parsley, chopped

Cook fettucini following package directions; drain. Melt butter; add cheese and parsley. Toss fettucini to coat with butter and cheese (waiters in restaurants make a big show of this). Arrange sausage alongside pasta on platter.

Sweet-Sour Red Cabbage

1 small head red cabbage	2 tablespoons sugar
3 tablespoons sausage or bacon fat	⅓ cup water
	½ teaspoon salt
1 tablespoon onion, chopped	⅛ teaspoon caraway seeds
4 tablespoons vinegar	Dash pepper

Remove outer wilted leaves; wash cabbage. Cut in halves; shred with large knife. Sauté cabbage and onion 3-4 minutes in hot fat. Add other ingredients; stir; cover; cook on low 3-5 minutes.

Melon Circles with Sherbet

Slice a honeydew or cantaloupe melon into circles; leave rind on. Remove seeds. Place one circle on each dessert plate; fill with lime sherbet.

In compelling man to eat that he may live,
Nature gives an appetite to invite him,
And pleasure to reward him.
         Brillant-Savarin

Polynesian Sandwich
Sautéed Tomatoes
Strawberry Frappe
(or purchased ice cream)

This is a super speedy meal if dessert is purchased.

Polynesian Sandwich

4 English muffins
8 slices canned pineapple
Thin sliced roast turkey

Sauce:
1 (10¾ oz.) can cream of mushroom or cream of chicken soup
½ soup can milk
¼ teaspoon sage
Salt and pepper to taste

Make sauce by heating soup, milk, and seasonings. Separate and toast muffins; place in shallow pan. Arrange turkey, then pineapple on muffins. Broil 2-3 minutes. Remove from oven; place on serving plate. Pour sauce over sandwich. Serves 4. Hint: A sliced kiwi fruit arranged around the edge of plate would be delicious and beautiful.

Sautéed Tomatoes

3 tomatoes, peeled and quartered
2 tablespoons butter
1 tablespoon cooking oil
1 clove garlic, mashed
½ teaspoon salt
Pepper to taste
½ teaspoon sugar
1 tablespoon lemon juice
2 tablespoons green onion, chopped
2 tablespoons parsley, chopped
2 tablespoons basil, chopped

If using dried parsley and basil, use only one tablespoon each. Heat fat on medium; add other ingredients. Sauté 2-3 minutes. Serves 4.

Strawberry Frappe

2 cups berries (fresh or frozen)
2 cups half-and-half cream
⅔ cup sugar
Dash salt

Mash berries, or run in blender. Combine with other ingredients. Freeze. Frappe should be served at mushy consistency.

Whatever hour God has given you for your weal, take it with a grateful hand, nor put off joys from year to year.

Horace, 23 BC

Tuna-Tomato Salad
Vegetable Finger Salad
(See Index)
Pretzels   Corn Chips
Pineapple Floating Island Custard

Tuna-Tomato Salad

4 medium tomatoes
1 (6½ oz.) can tuna
2 hard-cooked eggs
¼ teaspoon salt
Dash pepper

3 tablespoons mayonnaise
1 teaspoon lemon juice
2 tablespoons sweet pickles, diced
½ teaspoon dill weed
2 stalks celery, chopped

Combine all ingredients except tomatoes. Slice stem end from tomatoes. Cut each tomato into wedges, forming a star shape—do not cut all the way through the base. Sprinkle with salt; drain upside down.

Place each tomato on lettuce leaf; fill center with tuna mixture. Serves 4.

Pineapple Floating Island Custard

1 package vanilla or lemon pudding mix
1½ cups milk
Dash of ginger

Sliced pineapple, one per serving
Maraschino cherries

Mix pudding with milk and cook as directed on package. Pour into serving dishes. Float one pineapple slice on top of the custard. Put one cherry in the center of each pineapple slice. Cool in the refrigerator.

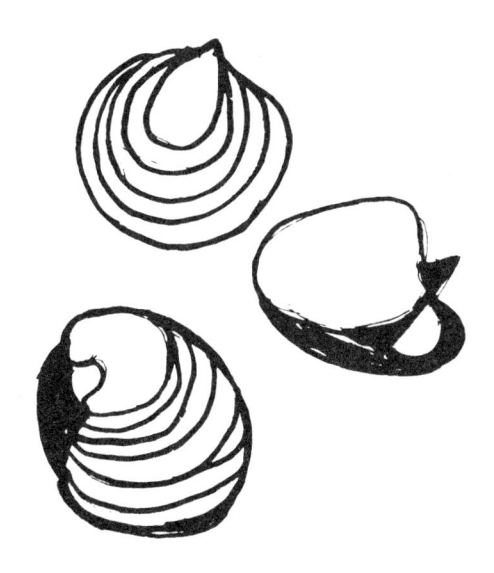

And above all things, have fervent charity among yourselves: for charity shall cover the multitude of sins. Use hospitality one to another without grudging.

1 Peter 4:8-9

Broiled Burgers
Hamburger Buns
Sliced Tomato, Onion   Potato Chips
Cookie Delight

A super speedy meal that even young members of a family would find fun to prepare. Most people will want mustard or catsup on their burger, so be sure to put those out.

The burgers could be formed ahead of time if desired. If they are prepared in advance, cover uncooked patties and keep refrigerated.

Broiled Burgers

1¼ pounds ground beef
1 tablespoon dried onion soup mix, or fresh onion

2 teaspoons Worcestershire sauce
¼ teaspoon salt
¼ teaspoon pepper

Mix all ingredients lightly. Shape into 4 patties. Broil 3 inches from heat 5 minutes; turn. Cook until desired doneness—4-6 minutes.

Cookie Delight

1½ **cups apple or fig bar cookies (cut cookies into ⅓ inch cubes)**
1 **cup whipping cream**

1 **tablespoon grated lemon rind or ½ teaspoon lemon extract**
1 **tablespoon sugar**

Whip cream; add sugar and lemon rind. Fold in cookie cubes. Pour into dessert dish. Serves 4-6.

The most costly outlay is the outlay of time.
         Antiphon, 430 BC

To save dishwashing time, keep a measuring cup in often-used dry ingredients such as sugar and flour. Also, keep a measuring spoon in the coffee can. No need to wash a spoon each time coffee is measured.

Ham and Herb Pancakes
Asparagus
Apple-Onion Salad
Orange Parfait

Substitute canned asparagus if fresh is unavailable. Warm; serve with butter and lemon juice.

Ham and Herb Pancakes

2-3 slices thin baked ham per serving
Pancake mix

1 tablespoon parsley, chopped
1 tablespoon chives, chopped
½ tablespoon thyme

Mix batter for pancakes, following instructions on box; add herbs.

Make large pancakes; spread while hot with butter. Stack six high with ham slices between cakes. To serve, cut like a pie, into wedges.

Asparagus

Wash well; break woody base off. Cook, uncovered, in salted water (1 teaspoon per quart water) 15-20 minutes.

Asparagus should be crisp when served. Pour lemon juice and butter over drained asparagus to serve.

Hint: A coffee pot is an ideal cooking utensil for fresh asparagus. Stand the vegetable upright (base end down) in the pot.

Apple-Onion Salad

2 red apples, cored; don't peel **¼ cup mayonnaise**
1 small onion, sliced into rings **2 tablespoons lemon juice**
¼ cup raisins **Salt to taste**

Toss ingredients; serve on lettuce. Serves 4.

Orange Parfait

Vanilla ice cream **½ cup orange marmalade**

Warm marmalade; pour over ice cream in parfait glass (easy elegance).

They eat, they drink, and in communion sweet/Quaff immortality and joy.

> Milton, Paradise Lost, 1674

Baked Chicken
Baked Potatoes
Kiwi-Apple-Grape Salad
Snowball

Put chicken and potatoes into the oven to bake one hour before you want to eat. That gives you an hour to do whatever you wish before dinner.

Baked Chicken

1 fryer (approximately 3 lbs.)
1 small onion
1 carrot
1 stalk celery

1 plastic baking bag
1 tablespoon flour
1 teaspoon salt
½ teaspoon pepper
½ teaspoon sage

Dust inside of bag with flour. Salt and pepper cavity of chicken; place carrot, onion, celery, and sage in cavity. Tuck wings underneath chicken. Place in bag; tie bag to close. Cut several slits in top of bag for air to escape. Place in shallow roasting pan. Bake in 350° oven 50-60 minutes.

Baked Potatoes

1 baking potato per serving **Margarine**

Scrub potatoes with brush. Rub margarine over skins; puncture each potato skin to allow escape of steam. Place on baking sheet. Bake 60 minutes.

Kiwi-Apple-Grape Salad
(A low-calorie, nutritious salad)

1 kiwi, pared and sliced **¼ cup cottage cheese per serving**
1 red apple, cored but skin left on **Red or green grapes**

Arrange on plate—alternating fruits. Add dollop of cottage cheese.

Snowballs

Ice cream (banana, peppermint, whatever flavor you like) **Shredded coconut**

Dip ice cream into balls; roll in coconut. Place in freezer on cookie sheet until serving time. Hint: If you want to keep snowballs prepared in freezer, just package in plastic bag. They keep for weeks.

Smoked Salmon on Lemon-buttered Toast
Stuffed Celery Rings
Cherry Tomatoes-Olives-Pickles
Date-Nut Ice Cream

A cooling summer meal which can be prepared ahead of time.

The colors and textures of this simple meal are beautiful. Place all the main course foods on one tray or individual plates so they can be appreciated.

Smoked Salmon on Lemon-buttered Toast

3 tablespoons butter
1½ teaspoons lemon juice
⅛ pound smoked salmon
4 slices sandwich bread

Prepare lemon-butter by creaming butter and lemon juice. Toast bread; trim crusts; spread with lemon-butter. Lay sliced smoked salmon on toast. Serve as open faced sandwich. Serves 4.

Stuffed Celery Rings

5 stalks celery
½ cup pimiento cheese or cream cheese-olive mixture

Wash celery; dry. Fill each celery stalk with cheese mixture. Take the smallest and next to smallest filled stalks; press together. Continue adding stalks of filled celery until a bunch is formed. Wrap in waxed paper; store in refrigerator until time to serve. At mealtime slice the cheese-celery bunch crosswise at half-inch intervals. You will have beautiful celery rings. Serves 4. If serving a larger group, use the entire bunch of celery, adding more cheese.

Date-Nut Ice Cream

1 quart vanilla ice cream
¼ cup nuts, chopped
½ cup dates, chopped
½ cup water

Simmer chopped dates and water 10 minutes; let cool. Soften ice cream slightly; add nuts and dates. Stir to distribute nuts and fruit. Keep frozen until serving time.

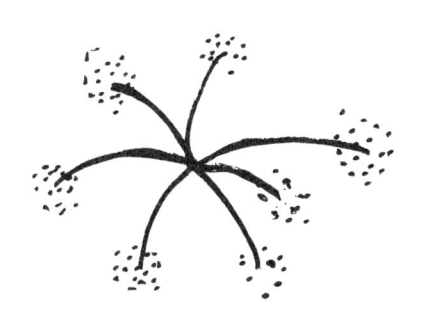

Better is a dry morsel and quietness therewith than a house full of sacrifices with strife.

Bronte, *Jane Eyre,* 1847

Franks in Cheese Sauce
Toast Points or Toasted English Muffins
(see Index)
Marinated Tomatoes
Sherbet

A hearty in-a-hurry meal.

Franks in Cheese Sauce

3 or 4 frankfurters
1 can (11 oz.) cheddar cheese soup
½ soup can milk
1 teaspoon dry mustard

Heat all ingredients; simmer 2-3 minutes. Serve over toast points or toasted English muffins. Serves 2.

Marinated Tomatoes

2 medium tomatoes
2 tablespoons salad oil
1 tablespoon vinegar
2 tablespoons parsley, chopped
1 clove garlic, minced
1 teaspoon dry mustard
Dash salt, pepper
Pinch sugar

Mix all ingredients except tomatoes. Peel tomatoes, then slice; place in bowl. Pour marinade over tomatoes; cover. Let chill in refrigerator until time to serve.

Time is often said to be money, but is more—it is life.
Avebury, 1887

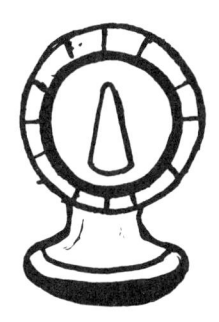

Save time when baking cake. Bake a sheet cake; top with sugar and spices or fruit topping. There will be one cake pan to wash and no frosting to make.

Save Clothes Washing Time

If clothes washer and dryer are near the kitchen, arrange to wash clothes while you are working in the kitchen.

If the washer is near bedroom area, plan to wash while cleaning that area.

Baked Tomatoes with Ham and Mushrooms
Coleslaw or Head Lettuce Salad
Chocolate Torte
(or purchase cake)

The main course is truly a one-dish meal and a wonderful use of leftover ham.

Baked Tomatoes with Ham and Mushrooms

4 medium-large tomatoes
½ pint fresh mushrooms, sliced
⅓ cup onion, diced
1 tablespoon butter
1 tablespoon cooking oil
½ teaspoon salt

¾ cup cooked ham, diced
½ teaspoon dill
1 teaspoon basil
1 tablespoon parsley, chopped
⅓ cup bread crumbs
Pepper to taste

Wash and drain tomatoes. Scoop out pulp; turn tomato shells upside down to drain. Sauté onions and mushrooms in fat 1-2 minutes. Add tomato pulp and bread crumbs, then other ingredients. Mix well; stuff into shells. Place into buttered baking dish. Bake 25 minutes in 375° oven.

Chocolate Torte

1 angel cake (10½ oz. loaf or round)
1 package (3¾ oz.) chocolate instant pudding mix
8-ounce nondairy whipped topping

1 cup milk
½ teaspoon vanilla extract
Chocolate fancies or chocolate curls

Slice cake into 3 layers. Place pudding mix, milk, and vanilla extract into whipping bowl; whip until stiff. Fold in nondairy whipped topping. Cover layers, sides, and top with mixture. Sprinkle top and sides with chocolate fancies. Keep refrigerated until serving time.

Time is but the stream I go fishing in.
Thoreau, 1861

Broiled Chicken
Broiler Green Peas   Broiled Tomatoes
(see Index)
Broiled Grapefruit

Broiled grapefruit makes a delicious appetizer or dessert; with this meal, it is used as dessert.

Cooking the entire meal requires one pan—the broiler. It takes little time to prepare or clean up.

Broiler Green Peas

Seasoning for the green peas is provided as seasonings drip from broiling chicken. You will need one can of green peas, any size desired. Place peas and liquid in bottom of broiler pan. Place broiler rack over peas. Follow directions below to broil chicken and grapefruit.

Broiled Chicken

2 chickens (1½ to 2½ lbs. each)
½ cup margarine
½ teaspoon soy sauce

2 tablespoons lemon juice
1 teaspoon salt
½ teaspoon sage, crushed

Wash, drain chickens. Cut each one into 4 sections or split in half lengthwise (chicken cut into 4 pieces cooks faster). Place on broiler rack.

Melt margarine; add other ingredients; brush fat mixture onto chicken. Broil 5 to 7 inches from heat—15-20 minutes on each side. Chicken is done when lightly browned and no pink shows if a drumstick is pricked. Serves 4-6.

Broiled Grapefruit

½ grapefruit per serving   Brown sugar

Slice grapefruit in half; cut out center, remove seeds; run knife around edge to loosen membrane. Sprinkle brown sugar on top. Broil until sugar melts. Serve warm with cherry in center.

Time is Eternity begun.

Montgomery, 1854

Crab-Mushroom Ragout
Ambrosia Salad
Vanilla Ice Cream with Chocolate Sauce

Ragout (ragoo′) is a highly seasoned stew. This one is super simple since mushroom soup is the basic sauce ingredient. It is time saving because there is only one cooking pan to wash.

Crab-Mushroom Ragout

1 can (10¾ oz.) cream of mushroom soup
½ can milk
1 tablespoon lemon juice
1 teaspoon dill weed
Dash pepper
½ teaspoon salt

1 cup crabmeat, flaked
1 can (2½ oz.) mushrooms
¾ cup sweet green peas, drained
1 tablespoon pimiento, chopped
Toast, English muffins, or patty shells

Make mushroom sauce by heating soup, milk, and seasonings. Add crabmeat, peas, and mushrooms. Stir gently; simmer 1-2 minutes. Serve over toast, split and toasted English muffins, or in patty shells. Serves 2.

Ambrosia Salad

1 orange, sliced into circles
½ cup grapes, stems removed
2 maraschino cherries

1 banana, sliced into circles
2 tablespoons shredded coconut
Lettuce

Place lettuce on salad plates; top with orange rings; add banana circles, then grapes. Toss coconut on top of fruit; add one maraschino cherry for color. Serves 2.

Animals feed themselves; men eat; but only wise men know the art of eating.

Brillant-Savarin, 1825

Chipped Beef Sandwich
Spinach Salad
(see Index)
Corn Chips
Melon Circles with Lime Sherbet
(see Index)

Chipped Beef Sandwich

This sandwich freezes beautifully. Make more than needed, freezing the extra ones for a planned over meal.

6 oz. cream cheese	**1 small jar dried beef**
3 tablespoons horseradish	**Butter or margarine**
1 tablespoon onion, minced	**White and whole wheat bread**

Trim crusts from bread; then butter all bread slices which will touch the beef-cheese mixture (this will prevent soggy bread). Each sandwich should have two white and one whole wheat bread slices.

Mince dried beef in blender or food processor. Add other sandwich spread ingredients; mix well.

Spread mixture on white bread; cover with buttered whole wheat bread. Spread beef-cheese mixture on top of whole wheat; add white bread. Cut each sandwich diagonally, forming triangles.

Eat now, or cover with damp (not wet) cloth and store in refrigerator; or freeze for future use.

When making cookies or biscuits, cut with a knife instead of a cutter. It takes three times less time.

Sweet-Sour Pork and Vegetables
Rice
Fortune or Almond Cookies
(purchase)

Sweet-Sour Pork and Vegetables

1 pound pork loin, sliced paper thin
3 carrots, cut julienned strips 2 inches long
½ cup onion, sliced
2 cups snow pod peas, fresh or frozen
4 tablespoons cooking oil

1 green pepper, cut ½-inch cubes
3 tablespoons soy sauce
6 ounces pineapple juice
½ teaspoon salt
½ cup water
2 tablespoons cornstarch
2 tablespoons cold water

Trim all fat from meat; place meat in dish. Sprinkle soy sauce over it; let stand 15 minutes. Place skillet or wok over medium heat; add oil. Add sliced onion; allow to soften; add pork in a single layer; cook until it loses pinkness. Add pineapple juice, salt, and water; cover. Simmer 3-5 minutes. Add carrots, snow peas, and pepper; stir-fry 2-3 minutes. Smooth cornstarch and cold water to a paste in a cup; stir into pork and vegetables. Stir constantly until mixture thickens. Serve with rice. Makes 4-5 servings. Green tea would be good with meal.

Nishime
Rice or Ramen Noodles
Prune Whip

Nishime

Nishime (nee-shee-may) may be cooked in a wok, electric skillet, or regular frying pan.

¾ pound raw chicken breast, sliced in ½-inch pieces
2-3 tablespoons vegetable oil
1 medium onion or ½ cup sliced green onions
1½ cups sliced raw mushrooms
2 cups snow peas (edible podded peas), ends and side strings removed
2 tablespoons lemon juice
1 tablespoon soy sauce

Heat oil; add onion, cook about one minute; add mushrooms and peas; stir-fry vegetables continuously one or two minutes. If using wok, push aside; if using skillet, remove vegetables to plate. Place chicken in pan. Sauté over medium heat 5 minutes, turning chicken so that it will all cook. Add lemon juice and soy sauce; stir. Return vegetables to pan; stir. Serve over rice or ramen noodles. Serves 4.

Prune Whip

4¾ oz. jar baby food, strained prunes with tapioca
1 egg white
½ cup whipping cream
1 tablespoon lemon juice
3 tablespoons sugar
Dash salt

Beat egg white and salt until nearly stiff; add sugar; fold in prunes. Without washing beater, whip cream; fold cream into prune mixture. Pour into sherbet glasses; serve cold. 4 servings.

Ripen bananas and avocados at room temperature.

Store-bought tomatoes have better flavor when allowed to ripen at room temperature, not in the refrigerator.

Cheese-Tuna Curry
Quick Parsley Rice
Tossed Green Salad
Fruit   Cookies
(purchased)

A full meal which could be prepared and on the table within thirty minutes.

Serve fresh, frozen, or canned fruit for dessert. Brown-and-serve French bread would be good with this meal.

Quick Parsley Rice

⅔ cup instant rice
⅔ cup water

2 tablespoons parsley (chopped)
¼ teaspoon salt

Boil water; add rice, salt, and parsley. Stir well; then cover. Remove from heat; let stand 10 minutes. Serves 2.

Cheese-Tuna Curry

1 can (11 oz.) cheddar cheese soup

1 can (6½ oz.) tuna
2 tablespoons sliced pimiento

¼ **cup milk** ½ **teaspoon curry powder**
1 tablespoon lemon juice

In a saucepan, blend 1 can cheese soup, lemon juice, and milk. Simmer; do not boil. Add drained tuna and pimiento. Stir; heat until warm.

Spoon rice onto platter, forming a ring. Fill center with Cheese Tuna Curry. Serves 2.

My son, eat thou honey, because it is good; and the honeycomb, which is sweet to thy taste.

Proverbs 24:13

Tomato Juice
Quick Chili
Crackers
Camembert Cheese
Fresh Pears or Apples

This chili can be cooked in 30 minutes or less, but it holds well on the stove for an hour or more. An ideal menu for a busy winter evening when the family has meetings, ball games, etc., they plan to attend and when they must rush out at different times. Prepare this nutritious meal; let each person serve himself if family members need to eat at different times.

Quick Chili

2 tablespoons margarine
4 stalks celery, sliced
1 small onion, sliced
1 clove garlic
½ bell pepper, sliced (if desired)
1 can (16 oz.) hot chili beans

½ lb. (more or less) leftover cooked beef or pork, chopped
¼ cup catsup
1 cup broth, bouillon, or water
½ teaspoon chili powder
½ teaspoon salt
¼ teaspoon cayenne pepper

Melt margarine in pan. Sauté onions, celery, bell pepper, and garlic in fat 3 or 4 minutes. Slightly mash chili beans; then add to vegetables in the pan. Add all other ingredients. Stir; then simmer 15-20 minutes. Serves 3-4.

Camembert Cheese and Fruit

Place wedges of Camembert cheese on a small tray. Place wedges of unpeeled fruit on tray.

Live with a thrifty, not a needy Fate;
Small shots paid often, waste a vast estate.
Robert Herrick, 1648

Deviled Ham-Cream Cheese Sandwich
Vegetable Finger Salad
(see Index)
Minted Applesauce   Cookies

An open faced sandwich which has meat, cheese, and vegetables on whole grained bread. A delicious meal in minutes.

Deviled Ham-Cream Cheese Sandwich

1 can (3 oz.) deviled ham
1 package (3 oz.) cream cheese
2 tablespoons pickle relish
2 tablespoons mayonnaise

Bean sprouts
Cherry tomatoes
Whole grained bread

Combine deviled ham, cream cheese, pickle relish, and mayonnaise.

Toast bread. (Use any type bread you like. I prefer round rye or whole wheat.) Spread ham-cheese mixture on toasted bread; add bean sprouts; top with cherry tomato—beautiful.

Minted Applesauce

2 cups applesauce
1 tablespoon mint jelly, melted

Maraschino cherries
Fresh mint leaves, if available

Combine applesauce and jelly; pour into compotes. Top each serving with one cherry and mint leaves. Serves 4.

Keep canned fruits in your pantry for quick salads or desserts—nutritious too.

Make out your market order before going to the grocery. Except for fresh fruit or vegetables, make only one trip a week to the grocery.

Keep a grocery list handy in the kitchen. Anytime someone opens the last container of a food, it is his or her responsibility to write it on the market list.

Quick Turkey Oriental
Rice
Raspberry Sundae

Quick Turkey Oriental

2-3 slices fresh turkey breast or boned chicken breasts
2 tablespoons cooking oil
1 (10 oz.) package frozen Japanese or Chinese style vegetables
1 tablespoon soy sauce

Slice turkey into narrow strips about ⅓ inch wide. Pour cooking oil into skillet or wok; heat to medium high; add turkey strips; stir-fry 3 minutes. Open vegetables; set aside seasoning pouch (in carton); add vegetables to turkey; stir well, cook following package directions. Add seasonings and soy sauce. Serve over rice. 2 servings.

Raspberry Sundae

½ cup raspberry jam
½ tablespoon lemon juice
Vanilla ice cream

Make ice cream sauce by heating jam and juice until melted. Scoop ice cream into serving dishes. Pour warm raspberry sauce over ice cream.

Seafood Fondue
Toast Points or Patty Shells
Seasoned Green Beans
Sliced Tomatoes
Maple-Nut Ice Cream

Seafood Fondue

1 (4¼ oz.) can shrimp
1 (4 oz.) can crab or lobster
1 (11 oz.) can cheddar cheese soup
1 tablespoon lemon juice
¼ cup milk
4 stalks celery, chopped
¼ cup bell pepper, chopped
2 tablespoons margarine
½ teaspoon dry mustard
1 tablespoon parsley, chopped

Sauté celery and bell pepper in margarine until crunchy tender (still crisp)—about 4 minutes. Turn heat to low; add soup, lemon juice, milk, mustard, and parsley; stir until smooth. Add seafoods; heat, stirring gently, until seafood is hot. Serve in baked patty shells or on toast points. Serves 2-3.

Toast Points

Toast sandwich bread. Cut each piece diagonally, forming triangle-shaped toast.

Seasoned Green Beans

1 can (16 oz.) green beans
1 tablespoon fat (butter or bacon drippings)
½ teaspoon seasoned salt
¼ teaspoon pepper

Drain liquid from canned beans. Melt fat in pan; add green beans, seasoned salt, and pepper. Sauté 3-5 minutes. Serves 4.

Maple-Nut Ice Cream

1 pint vanilla ice cream
⅓ cup salted nuts (chopped)
2 tablespoons maple syrup

Soften ice cream slightly. Blend in chopped nuts and syrup. Store in freezer until time to serve.

Thrift consisteth not in golde, but grace.
John Lyly, 1580

Corned Beef Roll-Ups
Hearts of Artichokes Salad
Sliced Tomatoes
Vegetable Finger Salad
(see Index)
Peach Puff
(see Index)

A cool-to-eat meal for a hot day. The roll-ups keep well for several days in the refrigerator. They also freeze well.

I like whole wheat crackers with this menu.

If in a hurry, purchase pie or cake.

Corned Beef Roll-Ups

1 package (3 oz.) wafer-thin corned beef
1 package (3 oz.) cream cheese
1 teaspoon lemon juice
1 tablespoon mayonnaise
1 tablespoon onion, minced
Dash Worcestershire sauce

Blend all ingredients except corned beef. Separate meat into stacks, two slices high. Spread with cream cheese mixture. Roll up each stack like a jelly roll. Freeze or allow to chill in refrigerator. Cut into one-inch pinwheel slices before serving.

Hearts of Artichokes Salad

1 can hearts of artichokes
Italian salad dressing
1 clove garlic, minced

2 tablespoons parsley, chopped
Salt and pepper to taste

Warm artichokes to boiling; drain off liquid. Add other ingredients and toss lightly. Marinate in refrigerator before serving; will keep several days.

He that gains time gains all things.

Samuel Palmer, 1710

Save trips to the grocery; keep basic food supplies on hand.

Pork Chop-Rice Skillet
Vegetable Finger Salad
Tutti-Frutti Ice Cream

This is an easy meal which can be put on to cook and left unattended until time to serve.

It is also a good meal to prepare days ahead of time. (The pork chop skillet and tutti-frutti ice cream freeze well.) Just warm the skillet meal and serve.

Pork Chop-Rice Skillet

4 pork chops
1 onion, sliced
2 cups canned tomatoes
½ cup rice, uncooked

1½ teaspoons salt
1 teaspoon pepper
1 green pepper, sliced
3 tablespoons fat

Brown pork chops in fat; drain fat from pan. Mix rice, tomatoes, salt, and pepper; pour over browned chops. Place sliced onion and pepper rings on top. Cover pan; turn heat to high until steam escapes from lid; turn to simmer. Cook 45 minutes to 1 hour. Serves 4.

Hint: To freeze for future use: Allow to cool in pan; place skillet and contents in freezer until frozen; remove food from pan; wrap for freezing. When ready to serve: Unwrap; place in same skillet; cover; warm.

Vegetable Finger Salad

Wash and slice fresh vegetables of your choice—carrot, zucchini, celery, radish, yellow squash—serve on tray with pickles.

Tutti-Frutti Ice Cream

1 pint vanilla ice cream
⅓ cup chopped, candied fruit

¼ cup coconut, if desired

Soften ice cream slightly. Add other ingredients. Store in freezer until time to serve.

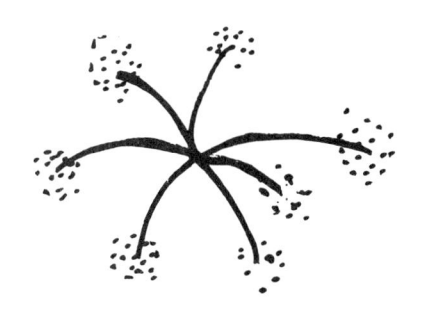

He who gains time gains everything.

> Benjamin Disraeli, 1847

If chopping food by hand, cut in bunches. Carrots, celery, green onions, etc. need not be cut individually.

Chicken Supreme
Rice
Congealed Cranberry Salad
(or canned cranberry sauce and sliced fresh fruit—apples, oranges, pears)
Sweet Potato Pie

This chicken lives up to its name—supreme.

The sweet potato pie is "out of this world" too. I always double the recipe when making it. One pie is eaten, the other frozen for a planned-over dessert. So much time can be saved when baking if recipes are doubled and frozen. Preparation pans need be washed only one time.

If pressed for time, purchase dessert, but do try this home cooked sweet potato pie sometime. I don't think you will be able to buy any pie half so good.

Chicken Supreme

4 supremes (boned chicken breasts from 2 fryers)
2 tablespoons butter or margarine
Salt and pepper to taste
¼ cup lemon juice
½ cup half-and-half or condensed milk
Parsley, chopped
½ pound fresh mushrooms, sliced
¼ cup green onion, chopped
2 tomatoes, peeled and chopped

Melt butter and oil in frying pan. Salt and pepper chicken fillets lightly. Sauté the supremes in fat 5-8 minutes on one side; turn the chicken and cook 5-6 minutes on the other side. They should be golden brown. Remove meat from pan; place on a platter.

Place onions, mushrooms, and tomatoes into fat remaining in the frying pan. Add lemon juice. Cook stirring continuously until fork tender (still crunchy). Slowly add ½ cup cream and parsley. Bring to simmer, but do not boil.

Place chicken on bed of cooked rice; pour the vegetable sauce over the chicken. Garnish with parsley, and sprinkle paprika on chicken. Serves 4.

Cranberry Salad

1 can (1 lb.) whole cranberry sauce
1⅓ cups water
1 package (3 oz.) raspberry or cherry flavored gelatin
1 orange
1 tablespoon lemon juice

Heat water; dissolve gelatin in hot water. Remove from heat; cool slightly. Add cranberry sauce to warm water, breaking it up with a fork. Add lemon juice.

Slice orange and remove seeds. Mince orange, rind and all, in food processor or blender. Add minced orange to other ingredients. Pour into mold. Chill until firm. Serves 4 to 6.

Sweet Potato Pie

Canned or fresh cooked sweet potatoes may be used. As with most vegetables, freshly cooked ones have more flavor.

1 cup mashed cooked sweet potatoes
¼ cup pineapple or orange juice
1 cup sugar
2 eggs, beaten
1 teaspoon nutmeg
½ teaspoon baking powder
1 teaspoon vanilla extract
¼ teaspoon salt

¼ **cup milk** **1 unbaked pie shell**
¼ **cup butter or margarine,
   melted**

Preheat oven to 400°. Mix all ingredients; pour into pie shell. Bake until golden brown on top—about 35-40 minutes.

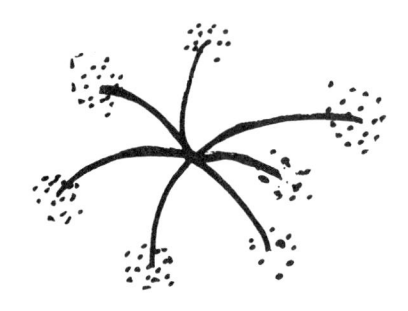

If any man hunger, let him eat at home.
1 Corinthians 11:34

Hurry-up Cake Decoration
Cover plain cake with paper doily. Sprinkle with powdered confectioners sugar. Remove doily; serve. A doily with large holes leaves a more attractive pattern than one with small holes.

Baked Fish Parmesan
Green Bean Casserole   Baked Apples
Apricot Pound Cake

To save time, turn oven on to start heating at 375°. Since apples take about 45 minutes to cook, start them first; add other foods at appropriate times so the whole meal comes out of oven together.

Baked Apples

2 apples
½ cup water, tinted with red food coloring
3 tablespoons sugar
1 teaspoon butter
¼ teaspoon cinnamon

Wash and core apples. Place in baking dish; pour water in. Fill centers with butter, sugar, and cinnamon. Bake uncovered about 45 minutes, basting occasionally.

Baked Fish Parmesan

6-8 oz. frozen fish fillets (perch, etc.), defrosted
1 (10¾ oz.) can tomato soup
2 tablespoons water
¼ cup Parmesan cheese
¼ teaspoon basil
¼ teaspoon salt
Dash Worcestershire sauce

In saucepan heat condensed tomato soup, water, basil, salt, and Worcestershire sauce.

Separate fish; place fillets in bottom of baking dish. Pour soup mixture over top. Sprinkle with cheese. Bake until done, about 25 minutes in 375° oven. Serves 2.

Green Bean Casserole

1 can (16 oz.) green beans, drained
1 can (10¾ oz.) cream of mushroom soup

1 can fried onion rings
Paprika
Salt to taste

Arrange green beans, then onion in buttered casserole dish. Spread soup on top. Sprinkle with paprika and salt. Bake in 375° oven 30-40 minutes—until bubbling. Serves 4.

Apricot Pound Cake

Pound cake (purchased)
Butter

Apricot preserves

Slice pound cake. Butter each side; toast. While the cake is warm, spread with apricot preserves and serve.

Nothing is ours except time.

Seneca

Baked Ham Slices
Fruit Buffet Salad
Marshmallow Salad Dressing
(or purchase dressing)
Peanut Butter Cake

Arrange thin sliced ham on one end of a platter. It is attractive to let slices overlap. Arrange fruits on other half of the plate.

A hot brown-and-serve bread would be good with this meal.

Fruit Buffet Salad

Honeydew or cantaloupe slices (chilled)
Orange slices or Mandarin orange segments
Grapes—red or green or both
Pineapple—fresh or canned
¼ cup salted nuts

Peel and slice melon into wedges. Place slices on tray. Arrange other fruits on top of melon. Sprinkle nuts on top. Serve salad dressing on side.

Marshmallow Dressing

1 cup marshmallow cream
3 tablespoons mayonnaise

1 tablespoon honey
½ teaspoon poppy seed

Whip marshmallow cream, mayonnaise, and honey in food processor or blender. Add poppy seed. Keep refrigerated.

Peanut Butter Cake

Yellow cake (purchased or homemade)

¾ cup peanut butter
¾ cup corn syrup (white)

Mix peanut butter and corn syrup over heat. Spread on top of cool cake. This will cover a sheet cake baked in a 7 x 13 inch pan.

Time is the one loan which even a grateful recipient cannot repay.

Seneca

Chicken Salad
Grapefruit Segments   Cranberry Sauce
Sesame Seed Biscuits
Sherbet and Pirouette Cookies
(purchased)

A simple salad meal with hot bread. The chicken salad could be made ahead of time and refrigerated until time to serve. It is a yummy use of leftover chicken or turkey.

Chicken Salad

2 cups cooked chicken, diced
1 cup celery, chopped
3 hard-cooked eggs, diced
1 tablespoon pimiento, sliced
¼ cup sweet pickle, diced
3-4 tablespoons mayonnaise
½ tablespoon lemon juice
¼ teaspoon salt
⅛ teaspoon pepper

Combine mayonnaise, lemon juice, salt, and pepper. Add other ingredients; toss lightly.

For each serving, dip a mound of chicken salad onto a lettuce leaf.

Slice cranberry sauce into circles, then cut each circle in half. Alternate one half-circle cranberry sauce with one grapefruit segment going all around the chicken salad mound. When complete the salad looks like a flower with cranberry sauce and grapefruit petals. Serves 4.

Sesame Seed Biscuits

1 can refrigerated biscuits
Milk

Sesame seeds

Roll each biscuit out (or use fingers to press out) about 1/8 inch thick. Brush milk on top of each biscuit; then sprinkle the tops with seeds. Cut each biscuit in half. Fold each half over the seeds, forming small folded biscuits. Bake in 475° oven 8 minutes or until browned. Serve hot with butter.

We mustn't waste time, for that's the stuff life's made of.
Benjamin Franklin, *Poor Richard's Almanac,* 1746

Shrimp Creole
Rice
Green Salad
Watermelon Slices

To serve this meal New Orleans style: Serve rice in individual bowls; dip the shrimp creole on top; eat with a spoon. French bread and black coffee would be good with this easy-to-prepare meal.

Shrimp Creole

¾ pound raw shrimp, cleaned, fresh or frozen
½ green pepper, chopped
3 tablespoons onion, chopped
3 stalks celery, chopped
2 cloves garlic, mashed
1 tablespoon cooking oil
3 tablespoons margarine
1 tablespoon cornstarch
1 (10¾ oz.) can tomato purée
¾ cup water
1 tablespoon Worcestershire sauce
½ teaspoon salt
⅛ teaspoon pepper
½ teaspoon each, parsley, basil, thyme
2 dashes red hot pepper sauce

Sauté green pepper, onion, celery, and garlic in fat. Cook until crunchy tender. Add cornstarch; stir until thickened. Add tomato purée, water, and seasonings. Cook over low heat 20 minutes, stirring often. Add shrimp; cook 10-15 minutes longer.

This recipe could be prepared ahead of time, adding the shrimp when heating sauce. Serves 2.

The proof of the pudding is in the eating.
                                    Henry Glapthorne, 1635

When chopping mint, lightly sprinkle with sugar. Sugar draws out the flavor.

Beefy Cheese Rarebit
Toast or Patty Shells
(purchased)
Sautéed Mushrooms and Peas
Pear-Berry Salad

No dessert needed with this meal. The fruit serves very well as salad and dessert.

Beefy Cheese Rarebit

1 (10¾ oz.) can cheddar cheese soup
½ (soup) can milk
1 (5 oz.) jar sliced dried beef (torn into strips)
½ teaspoon thyme
4 pieces toast, cut in half
Dash red hot pepper sauce or cayenne pepper

Heat milk and cheese soup; add beef and seasonings. Warm (but do not boil) 4-5 minutes. Pour over toast or patty shells. Serves 2 to 3.

Sautéed Mushrooms and Peas

1 small jar mushrooms
½ teaspoon sugar

1 tablespoon butter
1 can (17 oz.) sweet green peas
¼ teaspoon salt
Pepper to taste

Melt butter in pan; add drained mushrooms; heat 1 minute. Drain most of the liquid from peas; add to pan; sprinkle on salt, pepper, and sugar. Heat through, about 2 minutes.

Pear-Berry Salad

1 large pear half per serving
1 tablespoon berries (blueberries or strawberries, fresh or frozen)
Confectioners sugar

For each serving: place one pear half, cut side up, on lettuce leaf; fill center with berries. Sprinkle sugar on top.

Sit down and feed, and welcome to our table.
> Shakespeare,
> *As You Like It*

Ham and Asparagus Toast
Vegetable Tray
Cranberry Parfait

This parfait is so easy and delicious, you will want to keep some on hand in the freezer. When preparing it for a meal, dip parfaits up first; set them in freezer until serving time.

Ham and Asparagus Toast

4 slices cooked ham
1 small can asparagus spears (drained)
2 English muffins, split
1 tablespoon mustard
4 slices cheese (American or Cheddar)

Spread mustard on split sides English muffins; place on cookie sheet. Place one slice ham on each muffin half. Drain asparagus; arrange over ham. Cut cheese into one-inch strips; place over asparagus. Broil until cheese melts; serve hot. Serves 2.

Vegetable Tray

Slice fresh vegetables such as tomato, pepper, celery, carrot, squash, onion, etc. Place on tray. (A finger-food, high-vitamin salad in minutes.)

Cranberry Parfait

For an elegant-looking dessert, use stemmed parfait glasses.

Lemon sherbet　　　　　　　　**Whole berry cranberry sauce**

Place a small dip of sherbet into bottom of each glass. Add about one tablespoon cranberry sauce to each parfait, then another dip of sherbet; top with more cranberry sauce. Keep in freezer until serving time; better if slightly soft when served. If available, a dollop of whipped topping may be added at serving time.

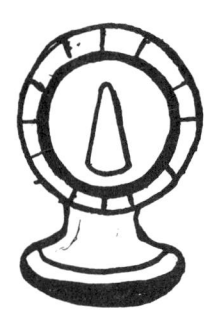

Time-Saving Hints

Remove stains from glassware by soaking in a mixture of vinegar and water. If that does not do the trick, soak overnight in false teeth cleaner.

Remove coffee and tea stains from teapots, cups, etc. by rubbing with baking soda moistened with water.

Remove mineral stains from china by rubbing with a mixture of salt moistened with water.

Tempting Seafood Casserole
Carrot Salad
Custard Pie

(Save time and energy; bake both dishes together. Make pie first. Bake in 475° oven 5 minutes; reduce heat to 400°; add casserole to oven.)

Custard Pie

2½ cups milk
4 eggs, slightly beaten
½ cup sugar

1 teaspoon vanilla
1 (9-inch) pie shell, unbaked
nutmeg to sprinkle

Scald milk; mix other ingredients. Pour hot milk slowly into mixture. Pour mixture into pie shell. Sprinkle nutmeg on top. Bake at 475° 5 minutes; reduce heat to 400°. Bake 15 minutes longer or until knife inserted into pie comes out clean.

Tempting Seafood Casserole

6-8 oz. frozen fish fillets
1 cup (8 oz.) canned green peas
¼ cup Parmesan cheese

Sauce ingredients:
1 (10¾ oz.) can celery soup
2 tablespoons water

¼ teaspoon dill
¼ teaspoon salt
2 teaspoons Worcestershire sauce
2 tablespoons parsley, chopped
Pepper to taste

Divide fish; place in bottom of casserole. Add drained peas. Mix listed ingredients to make sauce. Pour over fish and peas; sprinkle cheese on top. Bake 20 minutes in 400° oven. Serves 2.

Carrot Salad

2 carrots
½ cup raisins
1 tablespoon mayonnaise

2 tablespoons chopped nuts
Dash salt

Wash carrots; scrape; grate. Toss all ingredients. Serves 2-3.

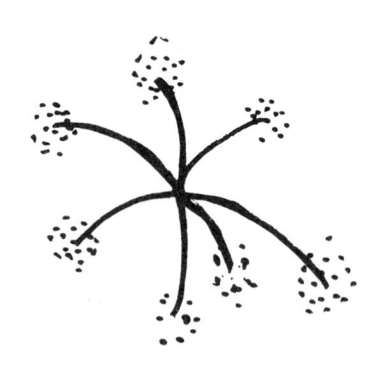

Unquiet meals make ill digestions.

Shakespeare, *The Comedy of Errors*

3

Essence of Herbs and Spices

Numerous books and articles have been written about growing and using herbs, yet to some people their uses seem a mystery. In fact, some writers imply there is a mystic formula for using them. Nonsense! Good cooks have known for centuries that tastefully used seasonings can give a gourmet touch to the simplest dish.

This book presents a host of quick-to-prepare foods, but you will note that the ingredient lists include many herbs and spices. Often it is the seasonings which transform simple foods into great, glorious meals.

Cooking with herbs is not complicated or time consuming. Their use makes food tastier and more appealing to the eye and appetite. Who can pass up an attractive dish with a heavenly-smelling aroma?

Let us spend a few moments thinking about seasoning terms.

1. *Herbs* are flowering plants with aromatic leaves or seeds which are valued for flavor, scent, or medicine.

2. *Spices* are pungent, aromatic plant products which are dried and used for seasoning. A spice might be made from seeds, bark, root, buds, flower parts, or fruit. Usually spices are grown in the tropics.

3. *Blends* are a combination of herbs and/or spices. They might be made with whole or ground seed mixed with

leaves or flowers. Curry powder is a blend of ginger, cloves, cumin, coriander, mace, cardamom, turmeric, fenugreek, black pepper, cayenne pepper, garlic, dill. All of these spices blend to produce the distinct characteristics of curry powder. With this combination it is easy to understand why a "little goes a long way."

4. *Fines herbes* [fen′ urby′ or fen′ zerb′] is a French term for an herb mixture containing equal amounts of finely chopped chives, tarragon, parsley, thyme, and chervil. It is a combination of delicate flavored herbs often used in soups, sauces, egg, and cheese dishes.

5. *Bouquet garni* [boo ka′ gar ne′] is a French term for a bundle of several herbs and spices cooked in a dish, then removed before serving. Bouquets garnis are most used in soups or stews when you want a blending of flavors. The most frequently used seasonings are parsley, leeks, bay leaf, thyme, basil, marjoram, peppercorn, and cloves. Most bouquets consist of three to five of the mentioned seasonings.

The fastest way to make a bouquet garni is to choose two to five herbs or spices; place them into a tea strainer; place the strainer into the cooking food for the last twenty minutes of cooking time. Remove strainer before serving.

The traditional bouquet garni is made by placing seasonings on a four-inch square of cheesecloth. Tie corners of the cloth together with string. Drop one bouquet into a pot of stew or soup. Remove and discard before serving. Several bouquets garnis can be prepared at one time. Store in a tightly covered jar until used.

Sensible Seasoning

1. Seasonings are to enhance flavors, not be the predominate flavor. When in doubt, use a small amount. Taste as you go; add more if needed.

2. There is no exact amount of herbs needed in a food. Tastes vary; therefore the amount of herbs one person finds delightful is too much or too little for another. Don't be

afraid to experiment. If you like it, you used the correct amount.

3. Most recipes call for dried herbs. (Of course if a recipe states to chop parsley, you know it means fresh parsley since you would not need to chop dried parsley.) If a recipe calls for a dried herb, and you have access to fresh, by all means use the fresh; just double the amount called for. Conversely if fresh is called for, and you wish to use dried, use half the amount called for in the recipe.

4. Too many herbs in a dish can be overwhelming, especially if several having strong flavors (i.e. oregano, dill, garlic) are combined. Strongly flavored herbs call for a light touch. When using them, it is better to let one herb be the principal seasoning.

5. Herbs are fragile. Store tightly covered, out of light, and away from heat. If they are purchased in a paper container, transfer to a metal or glass container which is airtight.

6. Test freshness of seasonings by giving them a sniff test. Open the container; the characteristic essence should greet you. If the herb or spice has a flat smell, toss it out and buy more. The flavor is gone.

7. Herbs usually keep top flavor for one year. It is a good idea to mark the purchase date on the container. Long storage causes flavor deterioration.

8. Most herbs are better if added the last ten to twenty minutes of cooking time. There is no need for long cooking; you just want to release the flavor.

9. Whole spices and seeds (cloves, peppercorns, etc.) need to cook longer to release flavor. Put them into food to cook the entire time.

10. Uncooked foods such as salad dressings and dips are best when seasonings blend with ingredients as long as possible. The flavors need to "marry."

11. To release the full essence of an herb leaf, crush it in your hand before adding to food.

12. Some seasonings lose flavor when frozen (salt, chives,

onion, etc.). Other seasonings increase flavor strength when frozen (imitation vanilla, pepper, cloves). It is a good idea to taste food which has been frozen to see if the dish needs a light touch of seasoning.

Herb and Seasoning Chart

On the next page is a simple chart which should be helpful to any cook, especially one who has little time to spend in the kitchen.

This chart is different from most since it first lists foods which you might be cooking, not herbs and spices. All a cook has to do is locate the food on the chart, then see what seasonings go well with it. This saves an enormous amount of time.

You will find the list most helpful when needing a substitute seasoning for one in a recipe. If you do not have a particular condiment, there is no need to run to the store. Refer to the chart; find the food; then see what other herbs or spices might go well with it. Choose one or two from the list. Do not use every one listed.

FOOD	HERBS	OTHER SEASONINGS	ADDITIONAL INFORMATION
APPETIZERS			
Cheese	Dill, Allium, Marjoram, Fines Herbes, Basil, Parsley, Thyme, Chervil	Worcestershire Sauce, Celery Seed, Paprika	Allium may be shallot, chives, onion, garlic, leek.
Meat, Beef, Pork	Basil, Savory, Dill, Thyme, Parsley	Mustard, Ginger, Worcestershire Sauce, Paprika, Cloves	Paprika is made from dried, ground red sweet pepper—a colorful garnish sprinkled on food. When cooked with food, it gives an aromatic, slightly sweet taste.
Poultry	Parsley, Chives, Sage, Basil, Thyme	Onion or Garlic Salt, Worcestershire Sauce, Celery Seed, Paprika, Turmeric	
Seafood	Dill, Parsley, Tarragon, Thyme	Celery Seed, Mustard, Lemon Juice, Cayenne	Celery seed is dried seed of celery plant. Celery flakes are dried leaves and stalk of the same plant.
Vegetable	Basil, Parsley, Savory, Thyme, Tarragon	Seasoned Salt or Pepper, Paprika	Easy vegetable dip: Combine equal amounts mayonnaise and sour cream; add 2 or 3 herbs and seasonings.
BEVERAGES			
Coffee		Cardamom, Nutmeg	Vanilla sugar is great in tea (hot or iced). To prepare: Split one vanilla bean open, cut into 1 inch pieces. Pour 1 cup granulated sugar over bean pieces. Keep tightly covered. Improves with age.
Fruit Punch	Marjoram, Mint, Rosemary, Saffron	Cinnamon, Cloves, Allspice	
Tea	Mint	Anise, Cloves, Lemon or Orange Juice	
CHEESE			
Quiche	Dill Weed, Thyme, Parsley	Paprika, Nutmeg, Curry, Ginger	Chopped pimiento gives flavor and color to cheese dishes.
Rarebits	Basil, Chervil, Parsley	Celery Seed, Paprika, Ginger	

FOOD	HERBS	OTHER SEASONINGS	ADDITIONAL INFORMATION
Sauce	Chives, Parsley	Paprika, Dry Mustard	Dry mustard gives zip to cheese dishes.
Soufflé	Basil, Chervil, Fennel	Paprika, Dry Mustard	
DESSERTS			
Cakes, Cookies	Saffron	Cinnamon, Mace, Cloves, Anise, Cumin, Ginger, Poppy or Sesame Seeds, Turmeric	Mace is the skin covering the nutmeg. Nutmeg and Mace are the only two spices which come from the same plant.
Custard	Bay Leaf, Thyme	Nutmeg, Cinnamon, Mace, Allspice	Mace can be substituted for nutmeg in recipes. I prefer mace in most fruit desserts.
Frozen Desserts	Mint	Mace, Cinnamon	
Fruits and Fruit Pies	Basil, Mint, Rosemary, Saffron	Anise, Caraway, Coriander, Cloves, Nutmeg, Mace, Cinnamon	
EGGS			
Creamed	Basil, Chervil, Tarragon	Dry Mustard, Paprika, Turmeric	Cumin is the ground seed of a plant in the parsley family. It is good with eggs, but strong and should be used sparingly.
Deviled	Basil, Chervil, Tarragon	Caraway Seed, Celery Seed, Cumin	
Scrambled or Omelet	Basil, Chervil, Tarragon, Marjoram, Fennel, Shallot	Celery Seed, Curry Powder	
MEATS			
Beef	Onion, Garlic, Parsley, Sage, Thyme, Basil, Bay Leaves, Chervil, Dill Weed, Marjoram	Celery Seed or Leaves, Seasoned Salts and Peppers, Worcestershire Sauce	Worcestershire sauce adds zest to most meats.
Lamb	Basil, Tarragon, Parsley, Dill Weed, Rosemary, Sage, Peppermint, Oregano, Thyme	Ginger, Curry, Dry Mustard, Cumin, Soy Sauce, Paprika	Create exotic dishes with lamb; use seasoning techniques of foreign lands such as Turkey and Greece.

FOOD	HERBS	OTHER SEASONINGS	ADDITIONAL INFORMATION
Pork	Sage, Basil, Marjoram, Thyme, Parsley, Onion	Soy Sauce, Dry Mustard, Catsup, Barbecue Sauce	Barbecue seasoning and soy sauce are especially good with pork.
Poultry	Sage, Marjoram, Thyme, Basil, Parsley, Rosemary	Soy Sauce, Lemon Juice, Dry Mustard	Herb cookery is great with poultry.
Seafood	Dill, Bay Leaves, Basil, Sage, Parsley, Tarragon, Thyme, Chives, Onion	Lemon Juice, Allspice, Curry Powder, Worcestershire Sauce	Dress up seafood before serving with a dash of paprika and chopped parsley or tarragon.
Veal	Basil, Dill Weed, Marjoram, Peppermint, Parsley, Rosemary, Leeks, Tarragon	Curry Powder, Lemon Juice, Parmesan Cheese	Veal is a delicate meat. Most people prefer light seasoning.
SALADS			
Fruit	Basil, Mint, Chervil, Marjoram, Rosemary, Onion	Cumin, Mace, Ginger, Cinnamon, Poppy Seed, Dry Mustard	A honey salad dressing for fruit salad is good with a dash of dry mustard and poppy seeds.
Green	Basil, Chervil, Parsley, Onion, Marjoram, Mint, Chives, Garlic	Parmesan Cheese, Paprika, Seasoned Salts and Peppers	Make herb vinegar by placing fresh herb sprigs into jars of cider vinegar. Set in the sun for one week, then in a cool dark place for one month.
Poultry	Parsley, Onion, Basil, Sage, Tarragon, Chives	Ginger, Paprika, Cayenne Pepper, Mustard	Tarragon-vinegar is good in fish sauces (tartar, etc.), seafood salads, and poultry salads.
Rice, Potato, Noodle	Basil, Dill Weed, Oregano, Parsley, Onion, Chives, Marjoram	Celery Seed, Dill Seed, Sesame Seed, Paprika, Poppy Seed	Lemon-thyme vinegar is good in mayonnaise and vegetable salad dressings.
Seafood	Basil, Dill Weed, Oregano, Parsley, Onion, Chives, Saffron	Lemon Juice, Worcestershire Sauce, Seasoned Salt or Pepper, Dry Mustard, Mace, Paprika	Chives and marjoram also make zesty salad vinegars.

FOOD	HERBS	OTHER SEASONINGS	ADDITIONAL INFORMATION
SAUCES			
Brown	Marjoram, Oregano, Sage		Sauces are to enhance food flavors, not overwhelm. Season with a light touch.
Cream	Chervil, Dill Weed (cream sauce for fish), Marjoram, Parsley	Paprika, White Pepper, Cayenne Pepper, Dry Mustard	Make cheese sauce by adding shredded cheddar cheese to basic cream sauce.
Tartar	Tarragon, Dill Weed, Onion, Parsley	Celery Seed, Chopped Pickles, White Pepper, Worcestershire Sauce, Dry Mustard	Dill weed is the preferred herb for tartar sauce.
Tomato	Basil, Bay Leaves, Marjoram, Oregano, Onion, Garlic, Thyme, Rosemary	Garlic Salt, Onion Flakes	Basil is a must for tomatoes. Chop it; use it fresh with sliced tomatoes; or cook it with tomatoes.
SOUPS			
Bean, Pea	Basil, Bay Leaves, Dill Weed, Oregano, Rosemary, Savory, Thyme	Cayenne Pepper, Cumin, Mace	Chopped celery and tomato are good in bean soup.
Clear Broth	Bay Leaves, Onion, Parsley, Thyme, Bouquet Garni	Parsley Flakes, Saffron (poultry), Cloves	Add chopped fresh parsley just before serving.
Vegetable	Basil, Bay Leaves, Chervil, Thyme, Bouquet Garni	Cayenne Pepper, Paprika, Celery or Parsley Flakes if not using fresh	Basil is the ideal herb for tomato soup.
VEGETABLES			
Artichokes	Basil, Bay Leaves, Dill Weed, Savory	Cayenne Pepper, Lemon Juice	Artichoke hearts are delicious marinated in Italian dressing.
Asparagus	Thyme, Tarragon	Lemon Juice, White Pepper, Dry Mustard, Paprika	Seasoned Hollandaise sauce is good on asparagus. Top with paprika.

FOOD	HERBS	OTHER SEASONINGS	ADDITIONAL INFORMATION
Beans, green or waxed	Basil, Dill Weed, Thyme, Onion	Nutmeg, Ginger	Ordinary vegetables become taste treats when properly seasoned.
Beans and peas—dried	Onion, Rosemary, Oregano	Cloves, Celery Flakes	
Beets	Peppermint, Dill Weed, Fennel, Bay Leaves, Thyme	Nutmeg, Ginger, Celery Seed, Mace	Nutmeg is especially good on glazed beets.
Broccoli	Oregano, Tarragon	Lemon Juice, White Pepper, Sesame Seed, Dry Mustard	A cheese sauce with celery powder is good on broccoli.
Brussels Sprouts	Dill Weed, Marjoram	Lemon Juice, Nutmeg, Ginger	Toss cold vegetable in Italian dressing.
Cabbage	Dill Weed, Oregano, Onion	Celery, Poppy, or Caraway Seed, Lemon Juice, Nutmeg	Do not overcook cabbage. It should be crunchy when served.
Carrots	Bay Leaves, Marjoram, Parsley, Mint, Thyme	Anise, Ginger, Allspice, Celery Seed	Brown sugar and mint go well with carrots.
Cauliflower	Basil, Rosemary	Nutmeg, Paprika, White Pepper, Sesame Seed	Cheese sauce with lemon juice makes a good topping.
Celery	Dill Weed, Peppermint, Thyme, Onion, Chives	Paprika, Lemon-Pepper, Sesame Seed, Dry Mustard	Sauté with onion; add dash of soy sauce for a quick vegetable dish.
Corn	Bouquet Garni in corn chowder; Basil, Rosemary	Pimiento or Sweet Pepper in creamed corn; Cayenne, Ginger	Add flavor to corn on the cob with herb butter.
Eggplant	Basil, Thyme, Oregano, Rosemary, Marjoram, Onion, Garlic, Sage	Fennel, Cumin, Allspice	Parmesan and Mozzarella cheeses are good in eggplant dishes.
Green Peas	Peppermint, Rosemary, Onion, Chervil, Thyme	Celery Seed, Sesame Seed, Ginger, Pimiento	Toss warm peas in lemon-butter; add mint; toss; serve.

111

FOOD	HERBS	OTHER SEASONINGS	ADDITIONAL INFORMATION
Lima Beans	Onion, Basil, Sage	Pimiento, Poppy Seed	Poppy seed gives a nutlike flavor.
Potatoes, White	Dill Weed, Basil, Tarragon, Onion, Chives	Celery Seed, Paprika, Mace, Nutmeg	When boiling potatoes, add dill weed the last 10 minutes of cooking time—delicious!
Potatoes, Sweet	Mint, Marjoram	Mace, Nutmeg, Ginger, Cloves, Cinnamon	Brown sugar and orange juice go well in sweet potato dishes.
Spinach	Marjoram, Basil, Onion, Chervil, Rosemary	Lemon Pepper, White Pepper, Nutmeg, Cayenne	Raw spinach and sliced onion rings makes a good salad.
Squash, Summer	Basil, Marjoram, Peppermint, Onion, Thyme	Cayenne, Celery Seed, Parmesan Cheese	Sauté with onion, celery, and basil.
Squash, Winter	Mint, Chervil	Nutmeg, Mace, Allspice, Cinnamon	Brown sugar and orange juice are good in many squash dishes.
Tomatoes	Onion, Chives, Garlic, Basil, Dill Weed, Tarragon, Fines Herbes	Mustard, Nutmeg, Ginger, Celery Seed or Flakes	Basil is called the tomato herb. Almost any tomato dish will be improved by adding basil.
Turnips, Rutabagas	Dill Weed, Marjoram, Oregano	Caraway Seed	To reduce the odor when cooking, add a little sugar to the water when boiling these vegetables.

Suggested Herbs and Spices to Keep on Hand
Allium (onion, shallot, garlic, or leek)—fresh, dried, or frozen
Basil—fresh or dried
Bay leaves
Celery seed
Chili powder
Chives—fresh or frozen
Cinnamon—ground and whole stick
Cloves—ground and whole
Curry powder
Dill weed—fresh, frozen, or dried
Ginger
Mace
Mint—fresh, dried, or frozen
Mustard—dry
Mustard—prepared
Nutmeg—ground
Paprika
Parsley—fresh, frozen, or dried
Pepper—
    Black peppercorns and mill (keep near stove for handy use)
    Cayenne—ground
    White—ground
Sage—fresh or dried
Salt
Thyme—fresh, dried, or frozen

4

A Balanced Diet—A Balanced Life

Total well-being is a worthy goal for ourselves and our families. This includes physical, mental, and spiritual well-being. A balanced life incorporates a balanced diet, exercise, and spiritual growth. "Whatever you do, whether you eat or drink, do it all for God's glory" (1 Cor. 10:31, GNB).

Good health habits are especially important for busy people because people on the run often snack a little here and snatch a little food there. Such eating might satisfy hunger, but not health needs.

The Balanced Diet

What is a balanced diet? A balanced diet supplies all the nutrients needed by the body to build and maintain body cells, regulate body processes, and supply energy.

One or two good foods a day are not enough. It takes a variety of foods—hence the balanced diet. Such a diet does not just happen, but neither does it require hours of preparation each day. If you will check the menus in this book, you will find an abundance of fresh fruits, vegetables, cheese, and meats. Milk is not listed as a beverage because beverage selection is left up to the reader. It is assumed that readers will drink milk daily as well as use it in cooking.

Foods needed each day are divided into four food groups—meat, milk, fruit-vegetable, and bread-cereal groups. Check yourself; do you eat a balanced diet?

Food Guide for Balanced Diet

FOOD GROUPS	ADULT* SERVING SIZE	AMOUNTS NEEDED DAILY
MEAT Group		
Lean Meat	2-3 oz. = 1 serving	Eat 2 servings daily for protein, iron, niacin, and thiamine.
Eggs	2 = 1 serving	
Peanut butter	4 tablespoons = 1 serving	
Dried beans and peas	¾-1 cup = 1 serving	
MILK Group		
Milk	1 cup = 1 serving	Adults need 2 servings
Yogurt	1 cup = 1 serving	Pregnant women need 4 servings
Ice Cream	1¾ cups = 1 serving	Children need 3 servings
Cheese	1½ oz. = 1 serving	Eat for calcium, riboflavin, and protein.
FRUITS and VEGETABLES Group		
Dark green vegetables	½ cup = 1 serving	Eat 4 servings daily from this group. One of these servings should be a source of vitamin C such as citrus fruit, melons, strawberries, tomatoes, greens.
Orange vegetables	½ cup = 1 serving	
Fruit juice	½ cup = 1 serving	
Fruit	½ cup or 1 medium = 1 serving	
BREAD and CEREAL Group		
Bread	1 slice = 1 serving	
Cereal		Eat 4 servings a day for carbohydrate, iron, niacin, thiamine.
Cooked	½ cup = 1 serving	
Ready-to-eat	1 cup = 1 serving	
Pasta	½ cup = 1 serving	

*Children need same number servings of Basic Four as adults. Serving sizes vary with age; the younger the child, the smaller the size serving.

Weight Control and Exercise

If you are overweight, you still need to eat the basic four foods. What you need to watch is how these foods are prepared and eating more food than you need. One raw apple has approximately 70 calories, while one slice of apple pie has about 345 calories. Watch the amount of fat (butter, margarine, salad dressing, fried foods) and concentrated, gooey sweets you eat. This doesn't mean that a person with normal health could never eat these foods; just watch the amounts eaten—limit them. Moderation in the amount of food eaten and regular exercise is the secret to weight control.

Exercise burns calories and strengthens heart and bones. If the exercise is enjoyable recreation, so much the better. Regular exercise and a balanced diet are essential for good health.

The Balanced Life

Set goals for a balanced life. Take time to:
1. Eat a balanced diet
2. Exercise regularly
3. Grow spiritually through meditation, service, and worship. "My brothers, fill your minds with those things that are good and that deserve praise: things that are true, noble, right, pure, lovely, and honorable. Put into practice what you learned. . . . And the God who gives us peace will be with you" (Phil. 4:8-9, GNB).

5

Company Coming

Most of us enjoy the company of others, but frequently feel we do not have the time or energy required for entertaining. Most likely we are dreaming of formal meals with difficult, time-consuming menus. Have you thought about preparing food days or weeks in advance, then storing it in the freezer or refrigerator until the day of the party? If you do this, food can be prepared whenever you have free time. There will be no last-minute rush to cook, freeing up time for you to touch up the house and possibly to relax a few minutes. It is wise not to exhaust yourself with preparation because people are coming to enjoy your company as well as the food.

A well-planned party menu has few foods which must be prepared the day you expect guests. Keep it simple; and if time is limited, purchase some food. Invite people with whom you want to share time; prepare one or two memorable dishes; serve them attractively, and you will have an enjoyable party—one which both you and your guests will enjoy.

An enjoyable party is one where people are relaxed, enjoying the food and conversation. It looks like it was easy to prepare, yet careful planning is the secret. Let's think about organizing yourself (schedule) so you too will have memorable occasions—large or small.

Planning for Company

First, ask yourself *what kind* of event you want to have. Will it be a rough-and-ready cookout for children, a Christmas dinner, or whatever? The kind of event you are having determines food and decorations.

Who will be coming? Be sure it will be a congenial group—people who will enjoy each other.

Where will you have it? There are all sorts of choices here. The dining room, kitchen, terrace, living room, and den are possibilities. If space is short, you might set up folding tables in the hall or bedrooms. If you think about it, the choices are extensive.

When will you have it? Be sure to think about your busy schedule and those of your guests.

What help will you have? Can you count on family or friends to help prepare food, serve, or clean up? If you can't, eliminate some of the work. Wise hosts are aware of limitations—time, energy, number of people they can comfortably serve. Keep it simple; guests would much prefer a relaxed host or hostess they can communicate with than all the elaborate food a French chef could prepare. A good casserole, salad, purchased bread, and dessert will do. Plan to let guests serve themselves buffet style. Use less tableware.

Do create a pleasant atmosphere for dining. The centerpiece, tableware, and linens should harmonize. They do not have to *match,* but they should *belong.* If you do not have complete sets of dishes, take a tip from clothing designers; use separates. Use pieces which are similar in scale and feeling yet different in color, pattern, or texture.

Company Cooking

You are having a party, but do not know how much food to prepare? *First,* plan your menu; or save time: Choose one from this book. *Second,* decide how many people you will serve. *Third,* see the chart on pages 119-120 to derive average amounts of food you will need to serve twelve or twenty-five people. The suggested amounts can be raised or lowered if you wish. After all, twenty-five teenage boys would eat more cake than twenty-five women. But rest assured; the suggested amounts can be relied upon for average amounts which will be consumed.

FOOD	AMOUNTS NEEDED	
	FOR 12	FOR 25
Meats		
Fish, with bone	6 pounds	12 pounds
fillet	4 pounds	8 pounds
Ham, uncooked, bone in	7 to 9 pounds	15 to 18 pounds
cooked, bone in	4 pounds	8½ pounds
boneless, cooked	3 pounds	6 pounds
Roast meat, uncooked		
bone in	5 pounds	9 to 10 pounds
uncooked, boneless	3 to 4 pounds	7 pounds
Meat, ground, uncooked		
beef or pork	3 pounds	5 to 6 pounds
ham loaf	1⅓ pounds ground ham and 2⅔ ground pork	2⅔ pounds ham 5⅓ pounds ground pork
Poultry		
chicken for frying	9 pounds	17 to 18 pounds
roast chicken or turkey, uncooked	10 to 12 pounds	18 to 20 pounds
Casserole	one 12-13 inch casserole	
Vegetables		
Carrots	3 pounds	5 to 6 pounds
Beans		
green, fresh	2½ pounds	5 pounds
green, canned	3 No. 2 cans	6 cans
green, frozen	3 12-oz. packages	6 12-oz. packages
lima, green, canned	3 No. 2 cans	6 cans
lima, green, frozen	3 12-oz. packages	70 ounces
lima, dried	1 pound	2 pounds
Broccoli	2 or 3 bunches	5 bunches
Corn, creamed, canned	3 No. 2 cans	6 cans
creamed, frozen	3 12-oz. packages	70 ounces
Mushrooms, fresh for cooking	2½ pounds	5 pounds
Peas		
green	3 No. 2 cans	6 cans
green, frozen	3 12-oz. packages	70 ounces
green, in pod	4 pounds	8 pounds

| FOOD | AMOUNTS NEEDED ||
	FOR 12	FOR 25
dried	1½ pounds	3 pounds
Potatoes		
white, mashed	4 pounds	8 pounds
sweet	4 to 5 pounds	9 to 10 pounds
sweet, canned	3 No. 2 cans	6 cans
Spinach		
fresh	4 pounds	8 pounds
frozen	3 12-oz. packages	6 packages
Squash		
summer, fresh	4 to 5 pounds	9 pounds
winter, fresh	4 pounds	7 to 8 pounds
Salads		
Carrots, to grate	2 pounds	4 pounds
Lettuce		
for salad cups	2 heads	3 heads
for salad	3 to 4 large heads	5 large heads
Slaw	2½ to 3 pounds cabbage	5 pounds cabbage
Tomato, sliced	4 tomatoes	7 to 8 tomatoes
Tuna fish	2 pounds	4 pounds
Desserts		
Cake	2 8-inch layers	3 8-inch layers
Cream for whipped topping	½ pint	1 pint
Ice Cream	½ gallon	1 gallon
Mints	½ pound	1 pound
Pie	2 9-inch	5 9-inch (some left over)
Salted nuts	¾ pound	1 to 1½ pounds
Strawberries	2½ quarts	4½ to 5 quarts
Beverages		
Coffee	1¼ to 1½ cups	½ pound
instant	½ cup in 2 quarts water	¾ to 1 cup in 1 gallon water
Cream for coffee	¾ pint	1½ pints
Hot Chocolate	3 quarts	5-6 quarts
Punch	1 gallon	2 gallons
Tea	1 dozen tea bags or ¼ cup loose	2 dozen tea bags or ½ cup loose

Centerpieces

When some people think of centerpiece decoration they think only of flowers. Floral arrangements are beautiful, but do consider other possibilities for decoration.

It is a good idea to keep in the house silk and dried flower arrangements which can be used in several rooms. When you are really rushed, these offer instant decoration.

All floral arrangements should harmonize in color and texture with the table service—any centerpiece should.

Objects other than flowers make attractive centerpieces. Some which are easy to set out are:

1. Tiered containers (dishes) which hold food to be eaten such as cheese, fruit, small cakes, cookies, candies.

2. A lazy Susan can serve the same foods. Place a few flowers or greenery around the food to add color and texture.

3. Shells, rocks, dried objects, candles, or unusual containers are just a few of the useful things you probably have around the house. Look around you; use common objects in uncommon ways. If you do this, you very likely can use your own things instead of making a spectacular purchase.

Ice Caper

Freeze mint leaves, sliced lemon, orange, and maraschino cherries in ice cubes. Keep fancy ice in freezer; add to tea or punch when needed.

Menus and Recipes

Food and decorations should be reflections of your own taste. I am suggesting some party menus here. This book also has numerous other menus which could be used for entertaining. Don't overlook the super speedy meals. They would do very well for drop-in guests or informal get-togethers.

Seated Dinners

When you are having guests for a seated dinner it is a good idea to have foods that are simple to prepare and serve—ones which can be mostly prepared ahead of time, so you won't be tired when guests arrive.

Let foods and decorations suit the occasion—formal or informal. One of my favorite menus for a prepare-ahead-of-time dinner follows on the next page.

Royal Chicken Bake
Baked Potatoes   Marinated Peas
Pickles, Olives, Radishes
Cranberry Ice
French Bread
(Purchase)
Quick Chocolate Cake

Royal Chicken Bake

This chicken is fit for a king. It can be prepared and cooked right away or it can be prepared for cooking, then left covered in the refrigerator overnight.

- 4 to 4½ lbs. chicken fryer breasts (Hint: I purchase split breasts with ribs when they are on sale and store them in the freezer until needed.)
- 1½ cups bread crumbs
- 1½ cups sour cream
- 2 cloves garlic
- 1 teaspoon celery seed
- 1 tablespoon parsley (or ½ tablespoon flakes)
- ½ teaspoon sage
- 1 tablespoon Worcestershire sauce
- 2 to 3 tablespoons lemon juice
- 2 teaspoons salt
- 1 teaspoon paprika

Rinse chicken in cold water. If chicken breasts are large, I cut each one in half. This is not necessary if you want to serve large pieces. The herb flavors seem to penetrate small pieces better than large ones.

Mix all ingredients *except* the chicken and crumbs in a bowl. Put bread crumbs in a bag. Dip each piece of chicken into the cream mixture; then toss it in the bread crumbs. Place in a shallow, oiled baking pan. When all the chicken is in the pan, cover it with foil wrap. Store in the refrigerator until ready to cook.

One to one and a quarter hours before you wish to serve it, remove from the refrigerator, uncover, and bake in a 350° oven. When done it is fork tender and brown on top—about 60 minutes. Serves 8.

Baked Potatoes

8 baking potatoes   **oil**

Scrub potatoes with a brush. Rub oil all over each potato. Puncture skin with a knife. Wrap all the potatoes in aluminum foil. Put into the oven to bake at the same time the chicken is baking. Time and fuel are saved by cooking two dishes at one time. Cook about 60 minutes or until soft. Before serving, roll each potato back and forth on a counter top to make it mealy.

Marinated Peas

2 cans garden peas
1 clove garlic, pressed
½ cup lemon juice or vinegar
½ cup salad oil

¼ cup sugar
2 tablespoons parsley
2 tablespoons dill weed
1 teaspoon salt

Drain peas. Place juice into a saucepan. Heat; add vinegar and sugar. Add peas to heated liquid. Empty into a glass container. Add all other ingredients. Put into the refrigerator. Serve cold. Drain liquid before serving. Serves 8.

Cranberry Ice

1 quart (1 pound) cranberries
1½ cups sugar
1 lemon, juiced

1 teaspoon plain gelatin
¼ cup water
1 egg white, beaten

Wash and stem cranberries. Cook with 1½ cups water in a covered pan until the berries burst. Put through a ricer to remove hulls. Cook pulp with the sugar until it dissolves. Dissolve gelatin in ¼ cup water. Add to pulp. Remove from heat; add lemon juice. Cool. Beat egg white; fold into cooled cranberry mix. Freeze. Stir several times while freezing.

This ice is tart and is delicious with poultry. Serve in small bowls with the main course.

Quick Chocolate Cake

1 angel cake
1½ cups whipping cream

⅔ cups instant cocoa mix

Cut cake crosswise forming 3 layers. Whip cream until nearly whipped; add cocoa mix; complete whipping.

Starting with bottom layer cover with whipped cream; stack the middle layer on next. Cover that layer with cream. Add the top layer. Frost cake with whipped cream. Keep in the refrigerator or freezer until serving time. If frozen, let sit at room temperature a few minutes before serving.

To feed were best at home.

Shakespeare, *Macbeth*

Broiled Lamb Chops
Broiler Green Peas   **Broiled Peaches**
(see Index)
Head Lettuce Salad
(see Index)
Sarah's Salad Dressing
Frozen Ice Cream Cake

A gourmet broiler meal which is partially prepared days in advance. The ice cream cake and salad dressing can be prepared at your convenience. Place the lamb chops, peas, and peaches on the broiler rack and in the pan before guests arrive. Run them under the broiler fifteen minutes before serving time. Pronto—dinner is served!

Purchased hard French rolls, butter, and beverage would complete the meal.

Broiled Lamb Chops

1 lamb chop per serving (cut ¾ to 1 inch thick)	Margarine Salt Pepper

Place lamb chops on broiler rack. Dot with margarine. Broil 2 inches from heat about 7 minutes. Turn chops over; dot with margarine; sprinkle lightly with salt and pepper. Broil to taste, approximately 6-8 minutes.

Broiled Peach Halves

Count on one or more peach halves per person.

1 can cling peach halves
1 teaspoon dry mustard
¼ teaspoon ground cloves
Dash of ginger

2 tablespoons brown sugar
Mint jelly
Butter

Drain ½ cup peach juice into bowl. Add brown sugar and spices. Place peach halves on broiler rack next to lamb chops, cavity side up. Pour spice and juice mixture over the peaches. Dot each cavity with butter, then ½ tablespoon mint jelly. Broil about 8 minutes.

Sarah's Salad Dressing

¼ cup blue cheese
½ cup mayonnaise
½ cup sour cream
1 teaspoon salt
½ teaspoon fresh ground pepper

1 tablespoon chives or green onion tops
1 tablespoon lemon juice
1 tablespoon parsley
1 tablespoon dill weed

This dressing is better if made ahead of time. It is good to keep on hand.

Frozen Ice Cream Cake

1 angelfood cake
1 pint strawberry ice cream
1 pint chocolate ice cream

1 quart vanilla ice cream
Coconut, toasted

Cut cake crosswise forming 3 layers. Remove ice cream from the freezer, allowing it to soften slightly. Starting with the bottom layer, cover it with a thick layer of strawberry ice cream. Stack the middle cake layer on top of the strawberry cream. Cover that layer with chocolate ice cream. Add the top cake layer. Frost the entire cake with softened vanilla ice cream (not melted).

If desired, toss toasted coconut onto the ice cream frosting.

Put into freezer until serving time. This is beautiful brought to the table and served. Let soften slightly before eating.

When at table, remember that we never repent of having eaten or drunk too little.

Thomas Jefferson, 1817

Buffet Service

When you are serving a large group, buffet service is usually the best. Since you can set all the food and drinks out, it allows you to entertain with ease. Let guests totally serve themselves, or pass hot bread and beverages after they are seated. If guests are eating at small tables, it is nice to serve the bread and beverages after they are seated—the bread will be fresh out of the oven hot.

Plan to use large trays [you might borrow some from friends] when guests will be sitting in various locations such as the floor, chairs, etc. A tray will hold plate, silver, napkin, and beverage (no balancing a cup on one knee and plate on the other).

Set clear traffic patterns, so guests can walk without bumping into furniture and each other.

If you are using a table for food service, and there is no space for beverages, use a small side table. Be sure to set out water as well as other beverages.

When the serving table is against the wall, a tall centerpiece is appropriate. It becomes a backdrop for the food. But if people will walk around the table, keep centerpiece low, so food and people can be seen.

No appropriate table for a buffet? Serve from a coffee table, tea cart, or kitchen counter; or cover folding tables with cloths and use them.

Easy Elegant Buffet
(for twenty-four)
Smoked Turkey
Baked Squash Casserole
Tomato Aspic
Hearts of Artichokes Salad
(see Index)
Vegetable Finger Salad
(see Index)
Hot Bread
(purchase and warm)
Ice Cream Pie

Smoked turkey can be readily purchased around Thanksgiving and Christmas. If you have difficulty locating one at other times of the year, go to a restaurant which smokes barbecue beef or pork. Very likely they will smoke a whole turkey for you. Slice the turkey; serve cold.

The squash casserole can be prepared ahead of time and put into the refrigerator until time to bake. It will rise higher if the eggs are added just before baking. Or you could bake the casserole, wrap, and store in the freezer. That way it could be baked weeks before the party. Thaw and warm before serving.

Prepare the salads a day or two in advance if you like. The artichokes are better prepared ahead.

Make the pie at your convenience. Slice and serve directly from the freezer.

Baked Squash Casserole

8-9 pounds summer yellow squash, sliced for cooking
1 bunch green onions (tops and all)
1 bunch fresh parsley
1 tablespoon fresh thyme
1 teaspoon salt
¾ cup water

Bring water to boil; add the above ingredients. Cover pan; cook on low until tender. Stir occasionally. Make cheese sauce while squash cooks.

Cheese Sauce

2 cans (11 oz.) cheddar cheese soup
1 soup can milk
¼ cup margarine or butter
½ cup cheddar cheese, shredded
⅛ teaspoon cayenne pepper
¼ teaspoon nutmeg
1 teaspoon Worcestershire sauce

Blend milk and soup over low heat until they form a smooth sauce; add other ingredients.

Drain squash; remove the onion and parsley. Mash squash slightly. Stir in cheese sauce.

Beat six eggs.

Blend eggs into squash mixture. Pour into one large or two medium casseroles which have been buttered.

Sprinkle top with grated cheese and breadcrumbs. Shake paprika on top. Bake in 350° oven until center of casseroles bubbles—30-40 minutes for medium size ones or 45-55 minutes for a large casserole. Serves 25.

Tomato Aspic

6 tablespoons gelatin
1½ cups cold water
9 cups tomato juice
⅓ cup onion, chopped
⅓ cup parsley, chopped

1 teaspoon salt
5 cloves
2 tablespoons sugar
1 teaspoon basil
⅓ cup lemon juice

Dissolve gelatin in water; set aside. Pour tomato juice into pan; add all other seasonings except lemon juice. Simmer 10 minutes. Remove from heat and strain. Reheat; add gelatin and lemon juice. Pour into mold; chill until set. Unmold on lettuce leaves and garnish as desired with pickles or olives. Serves 24.

Ice Cream Pie

For twenty-four servings you will need:

4 graham cracker crumb crusts
1 gallon vanilla ice cream
1 (8 oz.) can chocolate sauce

1 pint whipping cream, whipped
Maraschino cherries

Graham Cracker Crusts

5 cups graham cracker crumbs
¼ cup sugar

1 cup margarine or butter, melted

Combine ingredients into bottoms of four 9-inch pie pans. Bake in a 350° oven for 8 minutes. Remove from oven and cool.

Ice Cream Filling

Let ice cream sit at room temperature a few minutes until *slightly* softened.

Spoon ice cream into pie crusts. Drizzle pie tops with chocolate sauce. Put into freezer until serving time.

When serving, cut each pie into six slices. Top each slice with a dollop of whipped cream and a cherry.

He that eats well does his work well.
Scottish Proverb, 1721

Whipped cream will keep longer if a little plain powdered gelatin is added to it.

Use your freezer as a bank. When baking, double the recipe; then put extra food into the freezer for a planned-over dish. Withdraw when needed.

Buy food bargains and quick-to-prepare foods. Deposit for future use.

Quick Turkey Divan
Curried Fruit
Relish Tray
Coconut Spice Cake
(or purchase cake)

A great menu for a buffet meal. If you are having a dinner party, just increase amounts accordingly. A real easy elegance meal.

Turn oven to 350°. Put fruit in first; add Turkey Divan at appropriate time, so the whole meal comes out of the oven at the same time.

Curried Fruit

1 package (8 oz.) dried apricots
½ cup raisins
1 (16 oz.) can pears or peaches
3 oz. maraschino cherries (red or green)

1½ teaspoon curry powder
½ teaspoon mace
1 teaspoon ginger
2 tablespoons butter
½ cup brown sugar

Combine fruit and enough liquid to cover. Place in casserole. Mix spices and melted butter; pour over fruit. Cook 40-50 minutes. Hint: This fruit is good left over.

Quick Turkey Divan
(may be prepared ahead of time)

1½ cups cooked turkey or chicken, cut into 1 inch pieces
1 (10 oz.) package broccoli
1 (10½ oz.) can condensed cream of chicken soup
½ cup milk
½ cup cheddar cheese, grated
¼ teaspoon Worcestershire sauce
2 tablespoons lemon juice
¼ teaspoon salt

Cook broccoli according to package directions until just tender. Drain; place in bottom of 1¼ quart casserole. Lay turkey or chicken on top of broccoli.

In saucepan heat soup and other ingredients; pour over turkey and broccoli. Sprinkle paprika on top. Bake 20 minutes in 350° oven. Serves 4.

Relish Tray

Make an attractive arrangement of pickles, olives, and raw vegetables (carrot, celery, radish, avocado, squash, etc.) on serving tray.

Coconut Spice Cake

1 package spice cake mix

Prepare cake following package directions. Bake in 7 x 13 or two 9 x 9 pans.

Topping

1 cup brown sugar
¼ cup butter
1 cup flaked coconut
2 tablespoons milk

Combine ingredients. Spread over warm cake. Heat under broiler until golden brown.

Luncheons

Luncheons are usually given by women for women. Most menus feature light foods.

The type of service depends upon your home and guests. Food can be served wherever you like. The dining room, living room, and outside spots are nice service areas.

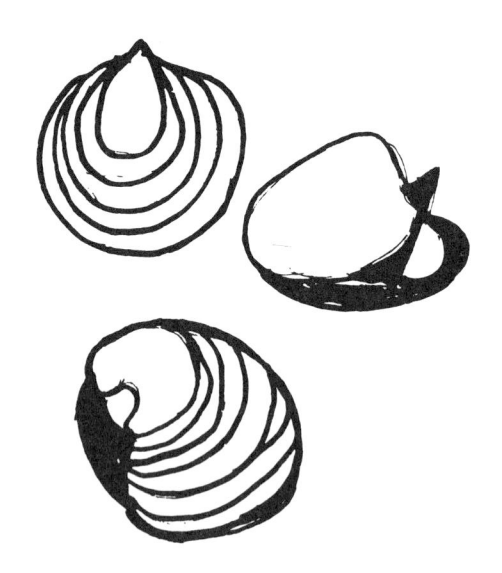

Better to eat onions with a tranquil mind than to dine on poultry with a troubled conscience.

Horace, 23 BC

Tuna Triple Decker Sandwich
Tomato-Avocado Salad   Corn Chips
Cherry Trifle

An ideal menu for a ladies' luncheon. The food is delicious and delightfully attractive.

No last-minute rush since the food can be prepared ahead of time. The sandwiches could be made and frozen days in advance or made the day before and left covered with a damp (not wet) cloth in the refrigerator. Wait until the day of the party to dip into nuts—so nuts will be crunchy.

Tuna Triple Decker Sandwich

18 slices sandwich bread
1 cup tuna, drained
1 (8 oz.) package cream cheese
1 teaspoon dill weed
Dash paprika
Butter or margarine

⅓ cup mayonnaise
2½ tablespoons lemon juice
1 cup salted nuts, chopped
1 (4¼ oz.) can ripe chopped olives, drained

Trim crusts from bread; then butter all bread slices which will touch the tuna mixture [this will prevent soggy bread]. Spread six bread slices with tuna mixture; cover with pieces of bread which have been buttered on both sides. Spread tuna mixture on top; add the third buttered bread slices.

Cut each sandwich diagonally into four triangles. Spread filling on inside cut edges of triangles. Dip spread edges into nuts. Serve with nut-topped triangles standing up. Makes six triple deck sandwiches.

Tuna Mixture

Combine mayonnaise, lemon juice, and cream cheese. Add dill weed, paprika, chopped ripe olives, and tuna.

Tomato-Avocado Salad

3 tomatoes, chilled
1 avocado, chilled
½ teaspoon basil

Salt and pepper to taste
Italian or French salad dressing

Peel and slice tomatoes. Peel and slice avocado. Sprinkle seasonings over vegetables; pour salad dressing over; toss lightly. Serves 6.

Cherry Trifle

An elegance with ease dessert. Prepare and serve it in a glass bowl, so everyone can enjoy its beauty. If you wish, make it hours before serving.

1 package ladyfingers
1 (5⅝ oz.) package vanilla pudding mix (not instant)
Jelly (your favorite)

1 can (16 oz.) pitted dark sweet cherries, drained
Whipped cream if desired

Split ladyfingers; spread tops and bottoms with jelly. Sandwich ladyfingers back together. Place ladyfingers in bottom of bowl and around sides of the bowl. (Stand them up like children holding hands and walking around.)

Cook pudding mixture, following package directions. Pour some of the pudding over ladyfingers in bottom of the bowl. Arrange a layer of fruit on top of the pudding. Repeat layers again. Top with fruit and whipped cream. Store in refrigerator until serving time.

Better cabbage with peace than sugar with grumbling.
Thomas Fuller, 1732

Tomato Bisque or Cream of Tomato Soup
(purchase)
Shrimp-Avocado Salad
Vegetable Finger Salad
(see Index)
Assorted Crackers
(purchase)
Quick Coconut Pie

A gourmet prepared-ahead-of-time meal—ideal for a luncheon. The only hot preparation is heating the soup before guests arrive.

If entertaining, you might serve cups of soup with crackers in the living room. Then move to the dining room where served salad plates await guests.

Shrimp-Avocado Salad

2 fully ripe avocados
1 can (5 oz.) shrimp, rinsed and drained
1 tablespoon lemon juice
3 tablespoons mayonnaise

½ teaspoon dill weed
1 tablespoon parsley, chopped
1 tablespoon onion, minced
Dash salt and pepper

Mix mayonnaise with lemon juice, dill weed, parsley, onion, salt, and pepper. Add shrimp. Set in refrigerator to chill.

When ready to serve, peel avocados; cut them in half lengthwise; remove seeds. Brush surface with lemon juice to keep color bright green. (If serving immediately, don't bother.) Fill avocado centers with shrimp salad. Serve on lettuce cup. Serves 4.

Quick Coconut Pie

1 9-inch pie crust
1 package (3¾ oz.) vanilla pudding mix (not instant)

¾ to 1 cup grated coconut
2 cups whipped topping

Bake pie crust; set aside. Cook pudding mix following package directions. Fold ½ cup grated coconut into hot pudding mixture. Pour into pie shell. Chill in refrigerator. Spread whipped topping over top of chilled pie. Sprinkle additional coconut on top. Serves 6.

A good dinner is worth more than a fine coat.
Isaac D'Israeli, 1820

Outdoor Entertaining

Patio parties can be as varied as a breakfast, a barbecue, or an alfresco dinner. All types are fun.

It is a good idea to limit what has to be carried out. Be sure that the food is portable. Use no more furniture than you and your helpers can easily handle.

To bring unity into a miscellany of different sized and shaped tables, use tablecloths and napkins of the same harmonizing colors. If flowers are blooming nearby, you might pick up their colors in the table settings.

Barbecued Chicken Drumettes
Baked Beans   Jalapeno Pepper Peas
Head Lettuce Salad
Cranberry Doughnuts

The chicken, beans, peas, and doughnuts could be prepared ahead of time, then put into the oven at the appropriate time to cook. Put the foods in the oven, set the table, cut the salad, maybe set out some crusty bread. Dinner is served—pronto.

Barbecued Chicken Drumettes

1½-2 pounds chicken drumettes
1 small onion, chopped; or 1 tablespoon dried onion soup mix
3 tablespoons lemon juice
½ teaspoon salt
1 teaspoon dry mustard
½ teaspoon celery seed

1 tablespoon butter
1 tablespoon Worcestershire sauce
2 tablespoons brown sugar
¼ teaspoon chili powder
⅔ cup catsup
⅓ cup water

Mix all ingredients except chicken. Place chicken in baking dish; pour sauce over it. Bake at 350° until tender—40-50 minutes. Serves 3-4.

Baked Beans

1 can (16 oz.) Pork and Beans
1 tablespoon bacon drippings
1 tablespoon brown sugar
3 tablespoons catsup
1 tablespoon onion, chopped or dried onion soup mix
Dash salt

Combine all ingredients. Bake in 350° oven until bubbling—30-40 minutes. Serves 3-4.

Jalapeno Pepper Peas

1 can (16 oz.) field peas
½ Jalapeno pepper, seeded and chopped
½ teaspoon sugar
1 tablespoon onion, chopped
1 tablespoon fat (drippings or butter)
¼ teaspoon salt

Combine all ingredients. Bake, covered, in 350° oven 45 minutes. Serves 3-4. Hint: Peas are also good cooked on stove top or in microwave—use whatever method is most convenient for you.

Cranberry Doughnuts

1 doughnut per serving
Cranberry sauce (whole berry or cranberry-raspberry)
1 (3 oz.) package cream cheese
2 tablespoons milk

Mix cream cheese and milk. Split doughnuts in half horizontally. Spread cream cheese on cut sides of doughnuts; add cranberry sauce. Sandwich doughnuts back together. Wrap in aluminum foil; heat in oven 2 minutes. Serve warm.

Head Lettuce Salad

Wash lettuce; drain. Cut into sections; place on salad plates; top with dressing.

Cold Cuts
Cold Vegetable Salad   Potato Chips
Hot Brown and Serve Bread
Ice Cream

A simple and simply beautiful meal for warm weather.

The vegetables are better when prepared ahead of time, allowing time for them to marinate in the salad dressing. Prepare and serve them in a glass bowl in order to enjoy their colors.

Cold Cuts

Place meat and cheese cold cuts on a tray, letting slices overlap. Add sliced tomatoes and pickles around the tray.

Cold Vegetable Salad

1 can (16 oz.) lima beans
1 can (16 oz.) or 1 pound cooked baby whole carrots
1 can (16 oz.) whole green beans
1 jar (4½ oz.) whole mushrooms

Salad Dressing:
½ cup salad oil
¼ cup vinegar
1 teaspoon salt
½ teaspoon freshly ground black pepper
2 tablespoons chives

**¼ cup parsley, chopped
1 teaspoon dill weed if desired**

Drain all vegetables; then layer them in a glass bowl. Start with lima beans on the bottom, then add a layer of carrots, then a layer of green beans. Top with mushrooms.

Combine salad dressing ingredients in a jar with a tight-fitting lid; shake well to mix. Pour dressing over the vegetables. Put into refrigerator to chill. Serves 12. Keeps well several days in refrigerator.

It isn't so much what's on the table that matters, as what's on the chairs.

Swift, 1711

6

Definitions of Cooking Terms

A la king
Food served in a rich cream sauce.

Appetizer
Beverage or small serving of food served as the first course of a meal.

Au gratin
Food with a browned covering, usually grated cheese or bread crumbs. Both cheese and crumbs might cover the top.

Bake
To cook in the oven. You might bake a cake or casserole. When applied to cooking meat it is the same thing as roast, which is cooking in the oven with dry heat.

Barbecue
To roast meat in the oven, or over coals, basting with a barbecue sauce.

Baste
To moisten food while it is cooking with juices from the pan, or a special sauce used for basting.

Beat
To blend vigorously with beater or by hand. Beating incorporates some air and blends ingredients well.

Blanch (or Scald)
To dip into boiling water, then (usually) into cold water.

Nuts, tomatoes, and some fruits are blanched to remove skins easily.

Blend
To combine ingredients thoroughly.

Boil
To cook until liquid boils and bubbles.

Braise
To sauté meat or vegetables in fat, then to cook with a small amount of liquid in a tightly covered pan.

Bread
To dip into egg or liquid, then to coat with crumbs, or flour before cooking.

Broil
To cook by direct heat. You may broil in a stove using a broiler pan or cook over coals.

Brown
To cook until browned in a small amount of fat.

Brush
To spread thinly (butter, egg white, etc.) with a brush.

Caramelize
To heat granulated sugar in a pan until it is browned. It must be stirred continuously.

Chill
To cool, but not to freeze.

Chop
To cut into small pieces—larger pieces than when minced.

Coat
To cover with a thin layer of nuts, flour, sugar, etc.

Coddle
To cook below the simmering point. To coddle eggs.

Combine
To mix ingredients thoroughly.

Cream
To beat one or more foods until soft and creamy—to cream butter and sugar.

Crisp-tender (or Crunchy)
   To cook until just tender, but not mushy or soft.
Cube
   To cut into squares.
Dice
   To cut food into small cubes.
Dredge
   To coat lightly with dry ingredients, such as flour or sugar.
Dust
   Same as dredge, perhaps with a lighter coating.
Dissolve
   To make a solution, or cause a substance to go into solution.
Drizzle
   To pour a threadlike stream over something.
Fat
   Butter, margarine, shortening, or animal fat such as lard.
Flake
   To break into small pieces.
Fold
   To combine ingredients without loss of air. This requires several motions: cutting down through the mixture, sliding the implement across the bottom, and bringing it up and over the top. One folds in beaten egg whites.
Fricassee
   To cook by braising.
Fry
   To cook in fat. Deep-fat frying is cooking in deep fat; pan-frying uses a small amount of fat.
Garnish
   To decorate food, usually with parsley, fruit, pimiento, etc.
Glace
   To cover with thin aspic, diluted jelly, or a thin sugar syrup.

Grate
 To cut into minute particles.
Grill
 Same as broil.
Grind
 To reduce to particles by crushing.
Julienne
 To cut into slender, long strips.
Knead
 To work dough by folding and stretching.
Marinate
 To let stand in a seasoned liquid.
Mince
 To cut or chop into fine pieces.
Mix
 To combine ingredients by stirring.
Pan-broil
 To cook on a hot surface, pouring off the fat as it accumulates.
Pan-fry
 Same as fry, using a small amount of fat.
Parboil
 To boil until partially cooked.
Parch
 To cook by dry heat. You parch peanuts in the oven.
Pare
 To remove the outside covering of vegetables or fruit such as apples or potatoes.
Peel
 To strip off the outside covering. One peels a banana.
Pit
 To remove the seeds.
Plump
 To thoroughly moisten and heat in the oven until full and round.

Poach
To simmer in hot liquid, being careful to retain shape of the food—to poach fish.
Purée
To make a smooth paste of fruit or vegetables. A food processor, blender, sieve, or ricer can be used.
Reduce
To boil liquid until part of it evaporates.
Render
To remove fat from meat by heating slowly until the fat melts.
Roast
To cook by dry heat. See bake.
Sauté
To cook quickly in a small amount of fat. Food is turned often while cooking.
Scald
To heat to just below the boiling point.
Score
To cut notches in food.
Scallop
To bake food in a sauce.
Sear
To brown the surface of meat quickly over high heat.
Shred
To cut or tear into small pieces.
Sift
To put dry ingredients, such as flour and baking powder, through a sifter or sieve.
Simmer
To cook on low heat. One starts vegetables in boiling water, then turns heat to simmer.
Skewer
To fasten meat, fish, or poultry with wooden or metal pins, so the meat holds its shape during the cooking process.

Sliver
> To cut nuts into thin pieces.

Steam
> To cook in steam with or without pressure.

Steep
> To soak in liquid below the boiling point. One steeps tea.

Stew
> To cook in liquid for a long time.

Stir
> To use a circular motion to combine ingredients.

Toast
> To brown by direct heat.

Toss
> To mix lightly.

Truss
> To tie meat so it will hold its shape. See skewer.

Until set
> When a gelatin mixture becomes firm.

Whip
> To beat rapidly to incorporate air and expand volume. One whips eggs, gelatin, cream, etc.

Let us now go home, for it is dinner time.
> Apocrypha, 166 BC

7
Weights and Measures

Dash = less than ⅛ teaspoon
Pinch = amount which can be held between thumb and finger. It is the same as "a few grains."
3 teaspoons = 1 tablespoon
1 tablespoon butter = ½ ounce
2 tablespoons = ⅛ cup
4 tablespoons = ¼ cup
5 tablespoons plus 1 teaspoon = ⅓ cup
8 tablespoons = ½ cup
½ cup = 4 ounces
16 tablespoons = 1 cup
1 cup = 8 ounces
1 cup = ½ pint
2 cups = 1 pint
4 cups or 2 pints = 1 quart
4 quarts = 1 gallon or 8 pounds
8 quarts = 1 peck or 16 pounds
4 pecks = 1 bushel or 32 quarts or 8 gallons

8

Food Equivalents

Apples: 1 pound, dried = 8 cups cooked
Apples: 1 pound fresh = 2 or 3 apples
Apricots: 1 pound, dried = 7 cups cooked
Apricots: 1 pound, dried = 3 cups raw
Bananas: 1 pound = 2 or 3 fresh
Beans: 1 pound, dried = 2 cups
Beans: 1 pound fresh = 1½ quarts
Bran: 1 cup = 1⅔ ounces
Butter or other fat: 1 stick = ½ cup or ¼ pound
Butter or other fat: 1 pound = 4 sticks or 2 cups
Cabbage: half pound = 2½ cups shredded
Carrots: half pound = 2 cups sliced
Chocolate: 1 square = 1 ounce
Cocoa: 2 tablespoons = 1 ounce
Cheese, cottage: 8 ounces = 1 cup
Cheese, cream: 3 ounces = 6 tablespoons
Cheese, grated: ¼ pound = 1 cup
Cream, whipping: 8 ounces = 2 cups whipped
Crumbs, graham cracker: 1 cup = 12 crackers
Crumbs, saltine: 1 cup = 17 crackers
Crumbs, vanilla wafer: 1 cup = 22 vanilla wafers
Cornmeal: 1 pound = 3 cups
Eggs, whole: 1 cup = 4 to 6 eggs
Egg, whites: 1 cup = 8 to 9 whites

Egg, yolks: 1 cup = 11 to 12 yolks
Flour, all purpose: 1 pound = 4 cups, sifted
Flour, whole wheat: 1 pound = 3½ cups
Flour, rye: 1 pound = 4½ cups
Lemons: 1 pound = 3 to 5 lemons
Lemons: 1 lemon = 3 to 4 tablespoons juice
Lemon, grated: 1 grated peel = 1 teaspoon
Macaroni, uncooked: 1 cup = 2 cups cooked
Marshmallows: ¼ pound = 16
Nuts, whole shelled: 1 pound = 3½ to 4 cups, chopped
Nuts, whole shelled: 5¼ ounces = 1 cup nut meats
Onions: 1 pound = approximately 3 cups
Orange, juiced: 1 orange = 6 to 7 tablespoons juice
Orange, grated peel: 1 orange = 2 teaspoons
Raisins: one 15 ounce package = 2½ cups
Rice: 1 cup uncooked = 3 to 3½ cups cooked
Spaghetti: 8 ounces = 5 to 6 cups cooked
Spinach: 1 pound = 2½ quarts raw or 1½ cups cooked
Sugar:
    confectioners: 1 pound = 3½ cups sifted
    brown: 1 pound = 2¼ cups packed
    granulated: 1 pound = 2 cups
Tunafish: ½ pound = 1 cup

Well cooked and seasoned and well talked, [the dinner] went very well.

Lucilius, 140 BC

9

Make Do

You are in a hurry to complete a meal; then you find you are missing an ingredient. Don't panic! Look at the list of substitutions suggested below. Lemon juice into sweet milk has helped me many times to get out a batch of biscuits when I wanted to make buttermilk biscuits, and there was no buttermilk in the refrigerator.

When you lack an herb or spice, refer to the herb and spice chart for suggested substitutions. For instance, you are cooking beef, and the recipe calls for an herb you do not have. Look at the chart to see what other herbs enhance beef. Be bold; try something new. Just don't try everything suggested in one dish!

1 tablespoon cornstarch = 2 tablespoons flour
1 cup sifted cake flour = 1 cup minus 2 tablespoons plain flour, sifted
1 cup plain flour = ½ cup plain plus ½ cup whole wheat flour *or* bran *or* cornmeal
1 cup sugar = ¾ cup honey
1 cup sugar (when baking) = ⅞ cup honey plus ⅛ teaspoon soda
1 square unsweetened chocolate = 1 tablespoon butter plus 3 tablespoons cocoa
½ cup fine bread crumbs = 2 slices day-old bread

2 egg yolks (in cooking) = 1 egg
1 cup buttermilk = 1½ tablespoons lemon juice or 1⅓ tablespoons vinegar in 1 cup sweet milk (let set 5 minutes)
1 cup sweet milk = ½ cup evaporated milk and ½ cup water
1 cup sour cream = 1 cup yogurt
1 cup skim milk = 3 to 4 tablespoons instant nonfat dry milk plus 1 cup water
1 cup half-and-half = ⅞ cup milk plus 3 tablespoons butter (for cooking only; don't whip)
1 cup heavy cream = ¾ cup milk plus ⅓ cup butter (for cooking only; don't whip)
1 cup butter = 1 cup margarine
   or = ⅞ cup lard plus ½ teaspoon salt
   or = ⅞ cup vegetable oil
½ tablespoon dried herbs = 1 tablespoon fresh
1 cup summer squash = 1 cup zucchini
1 cup corn syrup = 1 cup sugar plus ¼ cup water
1 cup sorghum syrup plus ½ teaspoon soda (reduce baking powder called for in original recipe) = 1 cup sugar
1 cup honey = 1 to 1¼ cups sugar plus ¼ cup water. (When sugar replaces honey in a recipe, replace sugar water cup for cup of honey, *but* reduce the other liquid called for in the recipe.)

Seven may be company, but nine are confusion.
                                          Thomas Fuller, 1732

He who dines well lives well.
                                          Horace, 20 BC

Index

Allium, see Herb and Seasoning Chart, 106
Ambrosia salad, 67
Angel cake, see
    in chocolate torte, 63
    in frozen ice cream cake, 127
Appetizers
    vegetable juice cocktail, 31
Apple(s)
    baked, 89
    in apple-onion salad, 55
    in kiwi-apple-grape salad, 57
    in kiwi-grapefruit-apple wedge salad, 22
    in Waldorf salad, 41
Applesauce
    minted applesauce, 77
Apricot(s)
    pound cake, 90
    whip, 26
    in curried fruit, 134
Artichoke(s)
    heart of artichoke salad, 83
Asparagus
    broiler, 16
    fresh, 54
    in ham and asparagus toast, 99
Aspic
    tomato, 132
Avocado
    in avocado-tomato salad, 138
    in shrimp-avocado salad, 140
    in tomato rose salad, 27
Baked
    chicken, 56
    royal chicken bake, 123
Balanced diet, see A Balanced Diet—A Balanced Life, 114
Banana
    boat salad, 43
    peanut butter salad, 44
    in ambrosia salad, 67
Barbecue
    chicken drumettes, 143
Basil, see Herb and Seasoning Chart, 106
Beans
    in cold vegetable salad, 145
    baked, 144
    chili beans
        in quick chili, 75
    green bean(s)
        broiler green beans, 25
        casserole, 90
        seasoned green beans, 81
    Italian green beans, 38
Bean sprouts
    in deviled ham-cream cheese sandwich, 77
    in sukiyaki, 35

Beef
    broiled beef burger, 52
    broiled steak, 25
    corned beef roll-ups, 82
    dried beef
        in beefy cheese rarebit, 97
        in chipped beef sandwich, 68
    minute steak-creole style, 44
    in quick chili, 75
    in sukiyaki, 35
    seasonings for beef, see Herb and Seasoning Chart, 106
Biscuits
    cheese biscuits, 23
    sesame seed biscuits, 94
Bouquet garni, see Essence of Herbs and Spices, 104
Bread(s)
    cheese biscuits, 23
    hot buttered pumpernickel slices, 28
    toast points, 80
    sesame seed biscuits, 94
Broccoli
    in quick turkey divan, 135
Buffet
    menus, see Buffet Service; also other menus in Meals in Minutes
    service, 129
Cabbage
    in sweet-sour red cabbage, 47
Cake(s)
    apricot pound cake, 90
    chocolate, quick, 125
    coconut spice, 135
    cranberry spice, 19
    frozen ice cream, 127
    peach puff, 34
    peanut butter, 92
Calories, see A Balanced Diet—A Balanced Life, 116
Cantaloupe
    in fruit buffet salad, 91
Caraway seed, see Herb and Seasoning Chart, 106
Carrot(s)
    julienne, 22
    salad, 102
    strips, 28
    in cold vegetable salad, 145
    in mandarin orange-carrot salad, 19
    in sweet-sour pork and vegetables, 70
Casserole dishes
    baked chicken salad, 31
    quick turkey divan, 135
    tempting seafood casserole, 101
Catfish
    scrumptious catfish, 33

158

Celery
    in stuffed celery rings, 58
    in sukiyaki, 35
Celery seed, see Herb and Seasoning Chart, 106
Centerpieces for table, 121
Chart(s)
    Definitions of Cooking Terms, 147
    Food, amounts needed for entertaining, 119
    Food Equivalents, 154
    Food Guide for a Balanced Diet, 115
    Herb and Seasoning Chart, 106
    Make-Do, 156
    Weights and Measures, 153
Cheese
    in beefy cheese rarebit, 97
    in c. tuna curry, 73
    seasonings for, see Herb and Seasoning Chart, 106
    cream cheese
        in chipped beef sandwich, 68
        in corned beef roll-ups, 82
    cottage cheese in tomato-c. cheese salad, 39
    pimiento cheese in cheese celery rings, 58
Cherry trifle, 138
Chicken
    bake, royal chicken, 123
    baked, 56
    barbecued drumettes, 143
    breasts, broiled, 64
    breasts of in nishime, 71
    curried chicken, 40
    curry, 40
    salad, 31, 93
    supreme, 86
Chili, quick, 75
Chipped beef sandwich, 68
Chocolate torte, 63
Coconut pie, 141
Coconut spice cake, 135
Coffee mousse, 38
Cold cuts, 145
Cookie delight, 53
Cooking terms, 147
Corn-filled tomatoes, 34
Cottage cheese
    in tomato rose salad, 27
    in tomato-cottage cheese salad, 39
Crab and crabmeat, also see seafood
    c. mushroom ragout, 66
    in seafood fondue, 80
    in seafood tomatoes, 23
Cranberry
    congealed salad, 87
    doughnuts, 144
    ice, 125
    parfait, 100
    spice cake, 19

Cream cheese
    in celery ring salad, 58
    in chipped beef sandwich, 68
    in corned beef roll-ups, 82
    in deviled ham-cream cheese sandwich, 77
    in tuna triple decker sandwich, 137
Curried fruit, 134
Curry
    cheese-tuna, 73
    chicken, 40
Custard, pineapple floating island, 51
Custard pie, 101
Date-nut ice cream, 59
Definition of Cooking Terms, 147
Dessert(s), also see cake, custard, fruit, ice, ice cream, and pie
    apricot whip, 26
    broiled grapefruit, 65
    cherry trifle, 138
    chocolate torte, 63
    coffee mousse, 38
    cookie delight, 53
    cranberry doughnut, 144
    honeydew melon, 32
    melon circles with lime sherbet, 47
    pineapple floating island custard, 51
    prune whip, 72
    strawberry doughnuts, 17
Deviled ham-cream cheese sandwich, 77
Dietary needs, 115
Dill, see Herb and Seasoning Chart, 106
Dinners, see Company Coming and Meals in Minutes
Doughnut
    cranberry, 144
    strawberry, 17
Dried beef
    in beefy cheese rarebit, 97
    in chipped beef sandwich, 68
Equivalents, table of, 154
Essence of Herbs and Spices, 103
Fettucini, 46
Fines herbes, 104
Fish
    baked fish parmesan, 89
    cheese-tuna curry, 73
    crab-mushroom ragout, 66
    scrumptious catfish, 33
    seafood fondue, 80
    seafood tomatoes, 23
    shrimp creole, 95
    shrimp soup, 42
    smoked salmon on lemon buttered toast, 58
    tempting seafood casserole, 101
    tuna-tomato salad, 50
Floating island custard, 51
Fondue, seafood, 80
Food Equivalents, 154
Food Guide For a Balanced Diet, 115

159

Franks in cheese sauce, 60
Frostings for cakes, see cakes
Frozen, also see ice, and ice cream
    f. ice cream cake, 127
Fruit(s), see: apple, apricot, avocado, cantaloupe, cranberry, dates, grape, grapefruit, honeydew, kiwi, orange, peach, pear, pineapple, prune, raisin, strawberry
    f. buffet salad, 91
    seasonings for, see Herb and Seasoning Chart, 106
Garlic, see Herb and Seasoning Chart, 106
Grape(s)
    in ambrosia salad, 67
    in fruit buffet salad, 91
    in kiwi-apple-grape salad, 57
Grapefruit
    broiled, 65
    g. segments with chicken salad, 93
    in kiwi-grapefruit-apple wedge salad, 22
Gravy, red eye, 30
Green beans, see beans
Green peas, see peas
Ham
    Broiled h. slice, 16
    fried country, 30
    h. and asparagus toast, 99
    h. and herb pancakes, 54
    in baked tomatoes with ham and mushrooms, 62
    in deviled ham-cream cheese sandwich, 77
    purchased sliced, in menu with fruit buffet salad and tomato-cottage salad (see salad)
Health, see A Balanced Diet—A Balanced Life, 114
Herb(s)
    blends and combinations, see Essence of Herbs and Spices, 103
    how to use, see Herb and Seasoning Chart, 106
    suggested h. to keep on hand, 113
Honeydew melon, see desserts
Ice, cranberry, 125
Ice cream, also see strawberry frappe, 49
    date-nut, 59
    maple-nut, 81
    peanut brittle, 28
    pie, 132
    strawberry cream, 41
    tutti-frutti, 85
    in coffee mousse, 38
    in cranberry parfait, 100
    in orange parfait sundae, 54
    in raspberry sundae, 79
    in snowballs, 57
Ice cream pie, 132
Icings, see cakes
Ingredient substitutions, see Make-Do, 156
Kiwi-apple-grape salad, 57

Kiwi-grapefruit-apple wedge salad, 22
Lamb, broiled chops, 126
Lima beans, see beans
Lobster, also see seafood
    in seafood fondue, 80
    in seafood tomatoes, 23
Luncheons, see Company Coming and Meals in Minutes, 15, 117
Make-Do, 156
Meat, see beef, chicken, fish, ham, lamb, pork, seafood, turkey, veal
Meat, seasoning for, see Herb and Seasoning Chart, 106
Melons, circles with lime sherbet, 97
    in fruit buffet salad, 91
Mint, see Herb and Seasoning Chart, 96, 106, 121
Mushrooms
    pan broiled, 21
    sautéed m. and peas, 97
    in cold vegetable salad, 145
    in crab-mushroom ragout, 66
    in sukiyaki, 35
Nishime, 71
Noodles, ramen, 40
Nutrition, see A Balanced Diet—A Balanced Life, 114
Onion, in apple-onion salad, 55
Orange
    in ambrosia salad, 67
    in fruit buffet salad, 91
    in mandarin orange-carrot salad, 19
Outdoor entertaining, see Company Coming and Meals in Minutes
Pancakes, ham and herb, 54
Parfait, see ice cream
Parsley, see Herb and Seasoning Chart, 106
Peach
    broiled, 127
    in curried fruit, 134
    peach puff, 34
Pear-berry salad, 98
    in curried fruit, 134
Peas
    field
        jalapeno pepper peas, 144
    green
        broiler green peas, 64
        marinated, 124
        steamed, 19
        in sautéed mushrooms and peas, 97
        in tempting seafood casserole, 101
    snow pod
        in nishime, 71
        in sweet-sour pork and vegetables, 70
Pepper, see Herb and Seasoning Chart, 106
Perch, see fish
Pies
    coconut, 141
    custard, 101

ice cream, 132
sweet potato, 87
Pineapple
  broiled, 17
  floating island custard, 51
  in fruit buffet salad, 91
  in Polynesian sandwich, 48
Pork, also see ham
  chop-rice skillet, 84
  sausage, 46
  sweet-sour pork and vegetables, 70
  seasonings for pork, see Herb and Seasoning Chart, 106
Potatoes
  baked white, 57, 124
  sweet potato pie, 87
Prune whip, 72
Pudding, pineapple floating island, 51
Ramen noodles, 40
Rarebit, beefy-cheese, 97
Red cabbage, see cabbage
Rice
  quick parsley r., 73
  in minute steak-creole style, 44
  in pork chop-rice skillet, 84
Salad(s)
  ambrosia, 67
  apple-onion, 55
  avocado-tomato, 135
  baked chicken, 31
  banana boat, 43
  banana peanut butter, 44
  carrot, 102
  chicken, 93
  cold cuts, 145
  cold vegetable, 145
  congealed cranberry, 87
  fruit buffet, 91
  head lettuce, 144
  hearts of artichokes, 83
  kiwi-apple-grape, 57
  kiwi-grapefruit-apple wedge, 22
  mandarin orange-carrot, 19
  marinated peas, 124
  marinated tomatoes, 60
  pear-berry, 98
  pink pear, 38
  relish tray, 135
  shrimp-avocado, 140
  spinach, 34
  stuffed celery rings, 58
  tomato aspic, 132
  tomato-avocado, 138
  tomato-cottage cheese, 39
  tomato rose, 27
  tuna-tomato, 50
  vegetable finger, 85
  Waldorf, 41
Salad dressing
  marshmallow, 92
  Sarah's, 127

Salmon on lemon-buttered toast, 58
Sandwich(es)
  chipped beef, 68
  deviled ham-cream cheese, 77
  ham and asparagus toast, 99
  Polynesian, 48
  smoked salmon on lemon-buttered toast, 58
  tuna triple decker, 137
Sausage, 46
Seafood, also see catfish, crab, fish, lobster, salmon, shrimp, tuna
  baked fish parmesan, 89
  s. fondue, 80
  s. tomatoes, 23
  tempting seafood casserole, 101
Seafood, seasonings for, see Herb and Seasoning Chart, 106
Sensible Seasoning, 104
Serving amounts needed for 12 or 25, 119
Shellfish, see fish
Sherbet, see desserts and ice cream
Shrimp, also see seafood
  s. avocado salad, 140
  s. creole, 95
  s. soup, 42
  in seafood fondue, 80
Soup, shrimp, 42
Spice cake, see cake
Spices, uses of, see Herb and Seasoning Chart, 106
Spinach salad, 34
Squash
  yellow, baked casserole, 131
Steak, see beef
Strawberry
  cream, 41
  frappe, 49
String beans, see beans
Sukiyaki, 35
Sweet potato, see pie, 87
Thyme, see Herb and Seasoning Chart, 106
Toast points, 80
Tomato(es)
  aspic, 132
  avocado salad, 138
  baked t. with ham and mushrooms, 62
  broiled, 26
  corn-filled, 34
  marinated, 60
  sautéed, 49
  seafood t., 23
  t. rose salad, 27
  seasonings for, see Herb and Seasoning Chart, 106
Tuna, also see seafood
  cheese-tuna curry, 73
  tomato salad, 50
  triple decker sandwich, 137
Turkey
  breast steaks I, 18

breast steaks, II, 21
  in Polynesian sandwich, 48
  in quick t. divan, 135
  in quick t. Oriental, 79
  smoked t., 130
Vanilla sugar, 28
Veal scallopini, 37
Vegetable finger salad, 85

Vegetable tray, 99, 135
Vegetables, listed by names
  Oriental style, in quick turkey Oriental, 79
  seasonings for, see Herb and Seasoning Chart, 106
Weight Control and Exercise, 116
Weights and Measures Chart, 153